MW00510704

Sassy Southwest Cooking

Vibrant New Mexico Foods
by Clyde Casey

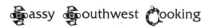

Copyright © 1997 by Clyde W. Casey
Cover Photograph Copyright © Mike Pettit
Graphics by RT Computer Graphics
Rio Rancho, NM 87174

This book may not be reproduced in whole or in part, by any means (with the exception of short quotes for the purpose of review), without permission of Clyde W. Casey.

ISBN 0-9659234-0-1
Library of Congress Catalog Card number pending

Published by:
Pecos Valley Pepper Co.
P.O. Box 2275
Colorado Springs, Colorado 80901

Printed by Alpha-Omega Printing, Inc.
Roswell, NM 88201

Cover Photo by Mike Pettit

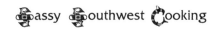

Dedication

To my wife of over 40 years, without whom my life would have no meaning. Millie is my companion, my partner, and always my love.

SASSY SOUTHWEST COOKING
Vibrant New Mexico Foods

INTRODUCTION

Since 1960 when I first traveled to New Mexico, I have been in love with its exciting cuisine. It is based on simple combinations of corn, beans, squash, game meat, chile, wild fruits and nuts. From the early 1500s when the Spaniards first arrived, this distinctive fare has been in a constant state of evolution. The result is a unique blend of many culinary arts that combine Native American, Spanish, French, Ranch Chuck Wagon, Mexican and Mediterranean influences. Today this rich savory cuisine is known world wide and each year millions of visitors to this "Land of Enchantment" learn to appreciate this festive food for the first time.

I hope that those who share my love of this sassy food will find these recipes worth trying. In my first cookbook, *New Mexico Cooking*, ISBN 1-55561-059-5, published by Fisher Books, I presented Southwestern flavors of the past and present. In this book I also present both traditional and modern dishes that will acquaint you with New Mexico's unique cuisine. Wild game and holiday dishes are also included; for those who are trying to reduce fat in their diets, many low fat recipes will meet their

needs. Few people are aware that New Mexico was making fine wines long before the planting of California's vineyards. Today these vineyards produce gold-medal wines.

With these recipes, you can experience the excitement of preparing bold-flavored foods. Share them with friends and family. There is no substitute for home--cooked-food: few if any, restaurants can capture the essence of this zestful food. The popularity of Southwest or Mexican-style food continues to grow and New Mexican dishes lead the way.

I believe recipes are to be shared and enjoyed. However, each must stand on its own. I have done my best to give you those considered special in one way or another. You'll find them interesting, pleasing to your palate and worthy of your effort. From the Land of Enchantment-*mucho gusto*!

Clyde W. Casey
Roswell, New Mexico

FROM GRAPE TO GLASS – New Mexico Winemaking

More than three centuries ago, as early as 1602, New Mexico vineyards produced wine from Mission grapes, making it the first wine-producing region in America. A century before wine-grape planting in California. In the 1880 census there were 3,150 acres of vineyards under cultivation in New Mexico, with an annual production of 905,000 barrels of wine per year. At that time, New Mexico ranked fifth among America's wine-producing states and territories.

The disastrous flood of 1897 followed by a severe drought convinced farmers to begin raising other crops. The final blow was Prohibition and by 1914 the Rio Grande Valley showed wine acreage to be a mere 8 acres. Bernalillo, known as the City of Coronado, is 18 miles north of Albuquerque. It was the center of New Mexico's wine production throughout the 18th and 19th centuries with up to 6,000 grape wine plantings reported in the 1870s. In his book El Gringo, published in 1875, W. H. Davis describes Bernalillo's clarets as better than French imports. The Christian Brothers monastic order operated a winery in Bernalillo until the 1950s and produced much of New Mexico's sacramental wines. The Italian Rinaldi and Gros wineries, late in the 18th century, and the French Mallet family winery, early in the 20th century, contributed to winemaking history in Bernalillo. The Mallet winery is still standing on the southern side of the Abenecio Salazar Historic District in Bernalillo.

In the 1970s and 1980s changes occurred in and around southern New Mexico in the Mesilla Valley. French, Italian, German and Swiss winemakers invested in New Mexico. Encouraged by the popularity of wines, they planted new vineyards all over the state. In 1990 New Mexico produced 700,000 gallons of wine, and today it has more than 5,000 acres of wine grapes. When today's acreage of vines mature, production will approach 4,000,000 gallons per year.

New Mexico vineyards flourish in different types of soils and at various elevations. Our soils range from deep clay loams over a rocky volcanic base in Southern New Mexico to shallow sandy loam in the northern part of the state. Elevations vary in the viticultural areas of the state: from 3,700 feet in the South up to 6,400 feet in the North.

While the Mission grape predominated in the early years of New Mexico wine making, it has gone by the wayside for the most part and only a few plantings survive here. Now, several varieties including both Vinifera in Southern New Mexico's warmer climate and the hardier French/American hybrids in the colder Northern part of the state or higher altitudes are thriving. New Mexico's climate is well suited for the growing of wine grapes. The arid desert climate with an average rainfall of less than 9 inches per year, combined with an extensive Rio Grande River irrigation network allow viticulturists to control the amounts of water needed to produce excellent grapes.

New Mexico experiences a phenomenon in grape growing that most desert regions do not. The sun is very intense because of cloudless skies. Also, the high altitude causes night time temperatures to drop 30-35 degree F. below daytime temperatures. Arid grape growing regions do not experience such contrasts in temperature. New Mexico's yields per acre are high; averaging 6 to 8 tons in a given season. Because of the long cool nights, vinifera and hybrids maintain a high acid to high sugar balance. A long growing season, intense sunlight, abundant irrigation, and most of all, the cool nights of the desert, all contribute to the making of good wines.

These are the types of vines and wines that are making New Mexico one of the premier wine growing areas of the nation.

VINIFERA

Chenin Blanc: Mesilla Valley and Mimbres Valley grow most of the Chenin Blanc grapes. Wines produced from this excellent white grape produce a fresh lively, fruity-light wine. Drier and finer, full and aggressive wines can be made from the Chenin Blanc grape. This wine compliments poultry or pork dishes.

French Colombard: A very prolific and vigorous growing white grape, excels in New Mexico. Because of its high-acid juice, it is used in making white wines and champagnes, and is a principal white wine grape in the Mesilla Valley. It's blended with other white wines, producing various light-semisweet wines. It goes well with appetizers, Monterey Jack cheese or chicken, and can be served as a dessert wine.

Merlot: Widely grown in the Mimbres Valley, it is considered a premium red-wine grape. It ages faster and has a softer, more delicate character than the Cabernet Sauvignon. Besides being a varietal wine, blending it with the Cabernet Sauvignon makes a fragrant, richly complex Bordeaux style wine. It is excellent served with wild fowl and Camenbert cheese.

Muscat: Muscat grapes, there are scores of different Muscat grapes, cultivated in southern New Mexico. All are spicy flavored. Muscat of Alexandria and Muscat of Blanc produce a most delicious, sweet, and low-in-alcohol wine. A dessert wine, Muscat Canelli, Italian for Muscat Blanc, goes well with cheese, apples and pears.

Riesling: Also know as White Riesling, produces some of New Mexico's most popular wine. It takes on a wide range of styles, from dry to sweet late harvest wines. Aromas and flavors of apricots and melons characterize its bouquet. Excellent for dinner with seafood or poultry as well as a dessert wine with cheese and fruit.

Ruby Cabernet: these red grapes flourish in the Mesilla Valley. This grape produces a powerful, astringent flavor, variously described as green olive, weedy and tannic. After its aged and bottled, it gradually loses its astringent taste and develops a

ꗊassy ꗊouthwest ꗊooking

fruity bouquet. An excellent wine to compliment beef or spicy foods.

Sauvignon Blanc: also know as Fume Blanc, it has adapted well to New Mexico's climate and soils. This white wine grape produces a distinctive, grassy, herbaceous-in-character, dry white wine. An excellent table wine to serve with seafood, fowl or vegetarian dishes.

Zinfandel: this big-red grape grows here and produces large, tight bunches, sometimes more than the vine can handle. It is one of our most widely planted varieties. Zinfandel, aged in wood and bottled for several years, develops a fine bouquet. White Zinfandels are gaining in popularity. They have an aroma subtly reminiscent of raspberry, which sometimes disappears with age. White Zinfandels are delightfully fresh, fruity and give off floral spicy aromas. Roses are excellent as sipping wines; and hardy reds are excellent with beef, lamb and spicy foods.

French-American Hybrids: northern New Mexico is well suited to the growing of these varieties. Both reds and whites generally tend to be soft and especially pleasant to drink young. A red that has developed a fine bouquet with cask and bottle is the Marechal Foch.

Baco Noir: another outstanding hybrid red with distinguished character. The flavor of its wine is as powerful as a Cabernet Sauvignon. The most popular hybrid white wine is Seyval Blanc. Northern vineyards and wineries specialize in growing and making wines from the French hybrids.

It is said that every stage of winemaking aims at the teaming wine with food which gives a whole different dining tempo—it creates a slower paced, relaxed dining experience.

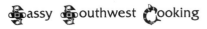

The New Mexico Vine and Wine Society and the New Mexico Wine Growers Association are the two groups who promote the wines of New Mexico. A free detailed map showing the location of wineries in the Land of Enchantment is available free by writing to New Mexico Wine Growers Association, P.O. Box 3511, Santa Fe, New Mexico 87504.

GOING WILD IN THE KITCHEN

Just as they did in the early days of this western land, hunting and fishing still provide an important portion of the menu of many New Mexicans. Although the wild buffalos no longer roam free, we have bear, elk, deer, and antelope to fill our freezers. Big game hunters come from all over the world for a chance to bag a trophy elk and deer from our bountiful meadows and pastures.

New Mexicans also hunt ducks, geese, wild turkey, pheasant, quail, dove and grouse for game birds. Bass, bluegill, carp, catfish, perch, Kokanee salmon and trout comprise the primary fish fare. Also actively hunted are rabbit, raccoon, squirrel and porcupine.

To a New Mexican hunter and fisherman, there is nothing that compares to the thrill of the chase. Golden aspen and the scent of the forest floor in autumn, the sight and sound of a flock of geese overhead or the distant bugle of an elk—these are what make the hunt special. Without them, hunting is no more exciting than a trip to the local supermarket. With them, the hunt becomes an indelible and mystical adventure. On those very special occasions when the game bag is bulging and the creel full with the harvest of the forest field and lake or stream, the hunter's family shares in the chase through the bounty provided by the hunter or

10

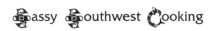

fisherman, just as the families of Native American hunters shared in the bounty before the Spaniards came to this enchanting land. Even in this day of scientifically designed foods, there is no fare to match the savory store from nature's pantry.

Fish and game, properly cared for and properly prepared, provide a variety of exciting dishes.

LOW FAT NEW MEXICO CUISINE

Like many other Americans, a growing number of us are becoming conscious of the fat content of our foods. New Mexican cuisine is based on beans, corn, squash, chile, and a large variety of fresh vegetables and nuts—is generally fat free. Because of the simplicity of the ingredients used, it is possible to retain the unique complexity, color, texture and creativity and still be lower in fat. Consider the bean a low-fat, protein-dense, easy to prepare, staple of New Mexico cooking. High in fiber and complex carbohydrates, without cholesterol, and inexpensive, beans make sense for everyday eating. There are many varieties available in a wide variety of colors, often in mottled patterns that are dotted or speckled. They are round, oval or flat, long and thin, or plump and kidney shaped. Their flavors range from the robust to hearty or earthy. Some are even delicate and subtle. New Mexican cooks are cooking with an ever broader selection of beans and pairing them with some unexpected partners. Our growers are experimenting with foreign and lesser known varieties and find that they enrich our nitrogen-poor soil. Try my Four Beans and a Pea Cassoulet for a special treat that is a great example of the use of these often underrated and overlooked legumes.

Corn, whether roasted, boiled, grilled, or steamed, can't be beat. American Indians have known its importance for centuries. They ate corn, beans, and squash and referred to them as the "Inseparable Sisters." This triad furnished them with an excellent nutritional balance. We can use this same trio today and enjoy the fat-free benefits they offer. Try the Indian Corn Casserole and see how well this trio works.

Attention should be directed to lean cooking methods; broiling, steaming, grilling, baking. The use of vegetable cooking spray and the selection of mono unsaturated cooking oils, such as Canola (rapeseed) and olive oil, should be strongly considered. Although I have added salt to most of the recipes, I like to use it sparingly and allow herbs to take a greater role in the flavoring and aroma.

It is much easier to control the fat content in typical New Mexican food because in many ways it is "peasant" food and its ingredients are very nutritious. The food producers are making more and more low-fat or no-fat products available to help in your food preparation. It seems that every time I visit the grocery market, I see a new item that offers low or no fat content.

The attractive part about preparing New Mexican food at home is that you can reduce the fat content. When you eat out, you have no idea what the fat content is and can bet it is prepared the quickest, easiest way. This usually means frying and the use of a lot of cheese and oil. If you are a lover of the vibrant flavors, colors, taste and textures of this cuisine, you will find that you do not to have worry—you can have your tortillas and eat them too.

NEW MEXICO: A LAND OF CELEBRATIONS

When pilgrims came ashore at Plymouth Rock, the first Thanksgiving had already taken place in what is now New Mexico, 23 years before in April 1598. According to historian Sheldon Hall, a party of 400 men plus perhaps 200 women under the leadership of Juan de Oñate, trekked across the barren expanses of what was then Northern Mexico. On the last four days they had no water and visions of exhaustion and death assailed them. These colonists finally came upon the Rio Grande del Norte. There, according to Gaspar Perez de Villagara, "they threw themselves into the water and drank as though the entire river did not carry enough water to quench their terrible thirst."

Within a few days they came in contact with the local Manso Indians and exchanged gifts and food. They thanked their deity and the generous Indians by holding a festive dinner, Mass, and a ceremony appropriating all the lands drained by the Rio Grande for the King of Spain. New Mexico is a land of mixed cultures. With such a diverse ethnic base, there is a constant flow of celebrations. The most dominant are the Native American, Mexican, and Spanish.

In this work I feature some of the dishes associated with these celebrations of life that are so much a part of this Land of Enchantment. I hope you like my choice of dishes.

TABLE OF CONTENTS

 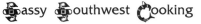

APPETIZERS

Having a party? Want to warm up your guests? Try a Habanero Salsa Cocktail. Add a dish of Portales Spiced Peanuts or some Chil-Eat-Zas and your guests will feel warm and welcome. In New Mexico Guacamole and Chile con Queso are old stand-bys. There are almost as many different recipes for these two as there are cooks who make them. I have included two excellent examples.

We have evenings that are warm and pleasant and a great many of us eat outdoors to enjoy the moderate climate. This offers an opportunity to serve appetizers and wine on the patio before dinner. In Santa Fe and many other of our cities, restaurants feature open-air dining. Shrimp Quesadillas or Stuffed Jalapeño Chile Peppers are both "winners," sure to please and might even help you to enhance your reputation as a great cook.

 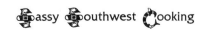

HABANERO SALSA COCKTAIL

Habanero is the hottest chile in the world. Be very careful in handling this pepper. Always wear rubber gloves and keep any of the pepper away from your eyes. This is hot stuff!!

4	**cups tomato juice**
2	**carrots, peeled blanched, chopped**
1/2	**habanero chile, seeded and chopped**
1	**tablespoon fresh cilantro, chopped**
2	**garlic cloves, minced**
1/2	**teaspoon salt**
2	**teaspoons honey**
	pineapple wedges for garnish

1. Place all ingredients except pineapple in blender and process at high speed until smooth.

2. Taste. If cocktail is too hot, add tomato juice as needed. Remember this one is for those who like it HOT.

3. Serve over ice in cocktail glasses. Garnish with pineapple wedges.

Makes 4 or more drinks.

The Institute of American Indian Arts Museum Located in Santa Fe, features the National Collection of Contemporary Indian Art. Its permanent collection Includes works by prominent artists such as Earl Bliss, T.C. Cannon, Darren Virgil Gray, Fritz Scholder, Doug Hyde Allen Houser, Charles Loloma and Kevin Red Star.

CHIL-EAT-ZAS

Quick and easy to prepare, surprisingly good to eat.

> 1   *lb lean ground beef*
> 1   *teaspoon vegetable oil*
> 1   *tube (10) refrigerator biscuits*
> 1   *can (7 1/2-oz) Mexican style tomato sauce*
> 2   *(4-oz) cans New Mexico green chiles,*
>   *chopped*
> 1/2 *lb. mozzarella cheese, sliced thin*

1. In skillet, brown beef in small amount of vegetable oil and drain. Set aside.

2. Preheat oven 300F(150F).

3. Separate biscuits and pat them out on a cookie sheet until they are flat circles. Spread tomato sauce on dough circles. Add layer of meat, then chiles and top with thin slices of cheese.

4. Bake for 15 to 20 minutes. Cut into quarters and serve hot.

Makes 40 appetizers.

Mozzarella cheese is a white cheese made from either whole or partially skimmed milk. It has a firm texture usually available in sliced, small round, or shredded form. May have preservatives added in "low moisture" varieties.

 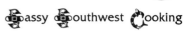

BLUE CORNMEAL PANCAKES

The heartier flavor of the blue cornmeal makes these pancakes unique and satisfying. The slate-blue color is impressive and different. A true New Mexico specialty.

1	*cup blue corn masa or blue corn meal*
1/2	*cup all-purpose flour*
1	*tablespoon sugar*
2	*teaspoons baking powder*
1/2	*teaspoon salt*
3	*tablespoons dry milk powder*
2	*eggs*
1-1/4	*cups milk*
2	*tablespoons vegetable oil*

1. In a mixing bowl, sift together the dry ingredients. In a separate bowl, beat eggs; add milk and oil and blend well. The batter will be a little thin.

2. Heat griddle over medium heat. Brush with a small amount of oil and cook pancakes at preferred size.

3. Serve pancakes hot.

Makes 4 servings.

Corn is the New World's single most important contribution to the human diet. Only wheat acreage surpasses it in number of acres planted. Columbus brought back corn with him to Europe and within a generation it was being grown throughout southern Europe.

CHILE CON QUESO

Triple this recipe for your next party and keep it warm in a crockpot. Serve with tortilla chips and watch it disappear.

2	*tablespoons butter*
1/2	*medium onion, chopped*
2	*garlic cloves, minced*
1	*tablespoon all-purpose flour*
1/3	*cup chicken broth*
2	*fresh tomatoes, peeled*
3	*New Mexico green chiles, roasted, peeled, seeded, deveined and chopped*
1/4	*teaspoon ground cumin*
	fresh ground black pepper to taste
8	*oz. Monterey Jack cheese, shredded or diced small*
3	*oz. cream cheese, diced small*
1/2	*cup heavy cream*
	flour tortillas

1. Make sure cheeses are at room temperature.

2. In small saucepan, melt butter; cook onions until soft. Add tablespoon of flour and stir for one minute.

3. In a food processor, combine tomatoes, chiles, cumin and black pepper until they are chopped, but not pureed.

4. Add mixture to saucepan and cook over medium heat about 4 minutes, add chicken broth; continue cooking until moisture has evaporated.

5. Remove the saucepan from the heat and stir in the cheese rapidly. When cheese is melted, add cream and thin to desired consistency. Do not overheat, or cheese will break down.

Serve with warm tortillas.

Makes 4 appetizers.

CREAM CHEESE CHILE DIP

This can be used as a spread or dip. It makes excellent stuffing for celery.

3	**fresh New Mexico green chiles, roasted, peeled, seeded and deveined, finely chopped, or 1 (4-oz.) can New Mexico chiles, chopped**
1	**(8-oz.) package of cream cheese**
2	**tablespoons milk**
1	**tablespoon white onion minced garlic salt to taste**

1. In a small bowl, combine all ingredients and beat until creamy, adding more milk as necessary.

2. Allow the dip to sit for at least one hour to allow the flavors to blend.

Makes 1 cup.

Cream cheese is a mildly tangy, smooth, creamy textured spreadable cheese. Developed in 1872 this soft unripened cheese is made from cows milk. Is sometimes sold mixed with Neufchatel to lower butter fat content.

DOUBLE CHEESE WHEEL

Here is an unusual combination of flavors. You will find it well worth the effort. A special dish for special occasions.

> 1   *lb. Chihuahua, Gouda or Monterey Jack cheese*
> 1   *(3-oz.) pkg. cream cheese softened*
> 1/4 *cup chopped, marinated artichoke hearts, drained*
> 1/4 *cup toasted pinon nuts*
> 1 1/2 *teaspoons chopped fresh basil or 1/2 teaspoon crushed dried-leaf basil*
>   *Crackers or tortilla chips*

1. If using Chihuahua or Gouda, remove wax coating or rind from cheese.

2. Hollow out cheese wheel with spoon or knife, leaving a 1/2-inch thick shell on the sides and bottom and set aside.

3. Finely chop removed cheese to measure one cup. Reserve remainder for other use.

4. Place chopped cheese, cream cheese, artichoke hearts, 3 tablespoons pinon nuts, and basil in a food processor and process until well mixed.

5. Pack mixture in the cheese shell and sprinkle with remaining pinon nuts. Press lightly.

6. Cover and refrigerate until firm, about 3 hours.

7. Cut into thin wedges and serve with assorted crackers and chips.

Makes 20 servings.

GREEN CHILE QUICHE

Here is a quiche with a sassy treatment. Serve as hors
d'oeuvre or a first course. Use your favorite salsa.

> 1 **(32-oz.) pkg. frozen "Southern Style" hash-
> brown potatoes, thawed**
> 1 **cup salsa**
> 1/4 **cup ranch dressing**
> 4 **eggs, lightly beaten**
> 1 **cup milk**
> 2 **(4-oz.) cans diced green chile peppers**
> 1 **cup shredded Monterey Jack cheese**
> 1 **cup shredded Cheddar cheese**
> **Sour cream**
> **Salsa**
> **Fresh cilantro**

1. Preheat oven to 450F(230C). Spray a 13 x 9-inch
   baking dish with a vegetable cooking spray.

2. Line a large bowl with several layers of paper
   towels. Place potatoes in a bowl, cover with 2
   layers of paper towels and press to remove excess
   moisture.

3. Spread potatoes evenly in bottom of prepared
   baking dish; bake in preheated oven 45 minutes or
   until golden brown.

4. In a small bowl, blend salsa with ranch dressing.
   In another bowl, mix eggs and milk.

5. When potatoes are cooked, remove from oven.
   Reduce heat to 350F(175C). Spread salsa mixture
   over potatoes. Pour egg mixture over salsa.

6. Sprinkle chile peppers over eggs; top with a layer
   of Monterey Jack cheese and then Cheddar cheese.

7. Return to oven and bake 45 minutes, or until
   cheese bubbles and is browned. Let stand 5
   minutes before serving.

8. Top each serving with sour cream, salsa and
   cilantro.

Makes 8 servings.

GUACAMOLE

My personal favorite. I use guacamole in many ways because it always adds special color, texture and taste.

2	*ripe avocados*
1/2	*teaspoon salt*
1	*garlic clove*
1	*teaspoon fresh lime juice*
1	*medium tomato, chopped*
1/4	*cup white onion, finely chopped*
1	*jalapeño chile, minced*
2	*tablespoons fresh cilantro, chopped*

1. Halve and pit avocados; place into glass or plastic bowl. Coarsely chop with two knives. Add salt and garlic then lime juice to taste.

2. Fold in tomato, onion, chile and cilantro. Allow flavors to blend for a few minutes before serving.

Makes 2 cups.

Although everyone seems to have their own method for making guacamole, the real secret is ripe avocados. Your avocado is ripe if it yields to light thumb pressure.

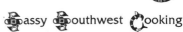

JALAPEÑO BEAN DIP

Why buy your dip from a market when it is this easy to prepare. Try it, and you will find there is no comparison in taste.

3	*ripe jalapeños, seeded and minced*
1/2	*cup green onion, diced*
1	*cup fresh tomatoes, peeled, diced*
2	*cups or 1 (15-oz.) can refried beans*
1-1/2	*cups Tomato Salsa (page #148)*
1/2	*cup black olives, pitted, sliced*
1	*cup cheddar cheese, shredded*

1. Preheat oven to 300F(150C).

2. In a bowl, combine all ingredients except 1/2 cup of the cheddar cheese. Mix well.

3. Place mixture in 8-inch baking dish. Sprinkle remaining 1/2 cup cheese on top. Bake 35 to 40 minutes.

4. Remove and place in serving dish.

Makes 6 servings.

 Jalapeño Chiles range from hot to very hot. Three inches long, they are green when immature and red when they ripen. Sold fresh, canned, or pickled they are the most famous chiles in the world.

LAS CRUCES DEVILED EGGS

Here you go. Deviled eggs with a sassy taste. Capers and cumin add interesting flavors.

12	*cooked eggs, peeled*
1/4	*cup mayonnaise*
1	*jalapeño pepper, seeded, finely chopped*
1	*tablespoon ground cumin*
1	*tablespoon capers, rinsed and finely chopped*
1	*tablespoon prepared mustard*
1/2	*teaspoon salt*
1/8	*teaspoon fresh ground black pepper*
	Ground red chile powder
	Fresh cilantro, finely chopped

1. Cut eggs lengthwise into halves. Carefully slip out yolks into a small bowl; mash with fork. Stir in mayonnaise, pepper, cumin, capers, mustard, salt and black pepper; mix until smooth.

2. Fill egg halves with egg yolk mixture, heaping lightly. Sprinkle with red chile powder. Garnish with cilantro.

Makes 24 eggs.

 Eggs are not only delicious as a food, but are used as a leavener in breads, cakes, and souffles. Long maligned because of their high cholesterol content, low cholesterol eggs are now becoming available in limited locations.

MUSHROOMS AND GREEN CHILES

An appetizing tray of these little shells is a welcome start to any New Mexican meal.

1/4	*cup butter*
3	*tablespoons green onions, finely chopped*
1/2	*lb fresh mushrooms, finely chopped*
2	*tablespoons all purpose flour*
1	*cup heavy dairy cream*
1/2	*teaspoon salt*
1/8	*teaspoon ground cayenne pepper*
2	*tablespoons canned green chiles, chopped*
1/2	*teaspoon lemon juice*
3	*tablespoons Parmesan cheese, grated and divided*
	Bread shells

1. In skillet melt butter, add onions. Stir constantly over medium heat for 4 minutes, without letting onions brown. Add mushrooms and cook for 10 to 12 minutes or until moisture is absorbed. Remove from heat.

2. Add chopped green chiles to mushrooms and sprinkle flour over mixture, stir well, and pour in cream. Bring to boil, lower heat, and simmer for 1 to 2 minutes. Stir in salt, cayenne pepper and lemon juice. Refrigerate.

3. Bread shells: Preheat oven 350F(175C). With a 3-inch cookie cutter, cut circles from sliced bread. Form shells by pressing bread into cups of small-sized muffin tins. Bake for 10 minutes.

4. Fill bread shells with mushroom chile mix. Sprinkle with reserved Parmesan cheese. Return to oven and bake for about 10 minutes

Makes 12 cups.

Sassy Southwest Cooking

NACHOS

New Mexico's contribution to fast food. Nachos are one of the most popular foods sold in convenience stores across the nation.

1 1/2   cups (6-oz.) Cheddar cheese
6   jalapeño chiles, seeded, cut into slices
Tortilla chips

1. Place tortilla chips on 4 small ovenproof dishes or a pie pan.

2. Sprinkle each with 1/4 of the cheese and 1/4 of the jalapeño slices.

3. Set oven to broil.

4. Broil about 3 to 4 inches from the heat until cheese is melted.

Serve at once

Makes 4 servings.

These are a great microwave food. Try garnishing them with lettuce, tomatoes, black olives, onions, or almost any vegetable. Sprinkle your selected garnish in and around the chips. Experiment with a variety of combinations.

NEW MEXICAN SPICED COFFEE

The national drink of Old Mexico is now catching on here in New Mexico. I like it better than cappuccino.

1/4	*cup boiling water*
3	*teaspoons instant coffee granules*
1/4	*cup brandy or cognac*
1	*teaspoon vanilla extract*
1/8	*teaspoon ground cloves*
1/4	*teaspoon ground cinnamon*
8	*egg yolks*
1	*cup confectioners sugar*

Garnish:
 whipped cream
 chocolate shavings
 cinnamon sticks

1. In small bowl, pour boiling water to instant coffee. Add brandy, vanilla, cloves and cinnamon. Set aside.

2. In a double boiler, over simmering water, beat the egg yolks and sugar until light and foamy. Beating continuously, slowly add coffee until mixture doubles in bulk and thickens.

3. Spoon into serving glasses. Garnish with whipped cream, shaved chocolate and a cinnamon stick. Serve immediately.

Makes 4 to 6 servings.

PORTALES SPICED PEANUTS

No one I know can eat just one of these. An ideal snack, be prepared for them to disappear quickly.

2	*teaspoons peanut oil*
4	*cloves garlic, crushed*
2	*cups unsalted dry-roasted Valencia red peanuts*
2	*tablespoons chili powder*
1/2	*teaspoon salt*

1. In a large skillet heat oil over medium heat. Cook garlic stirring occasionally until golden brown; remove garlic and discard.

2. Add chili powder and peanuts and cook over medium heat for about 2 minutes, stirring occasionally, until peanuts are very warm. Remove peanuts and drain. While still warm sprinkle with salt. Cool.

Makes 2 cups.

Peanuts are an important cash crop in New Mexico. The peanut is actually a legume not a nut, true nuts grow on trees. They are also called, goobers, groundnuts or monkey nuts, because after flowering, the plant bends down to the earth and its pod ripens underground.

 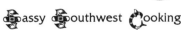

SHRIMP QUESADILLAS

If you are looking for a special appetizer with a New Mexican touch, look no further.

4	*tablespoons butter*
4	*(10-inch) flour tortilla*
1/2	*cup Cheddar cheese, shredded*
1/2	*cup Monterey Jack cheese, shredded*
2	*jalapeño chiles, seeded, deveined, sliced*
16	*shrimp, shelled, cooked, sliced in half lengthwise*
4	*tablespoons dairy sour cream*
1	*large tomato, chopped*
2	*ripe avocados, peeled, sliced*
	Paprika

1. Preheat oven to 350F(175C).

2. Lightly butter one side of tortilla. Place buttered side down, on flat cookie sheet.

3. On each of the 4 tortillas spread cheeses to within 1/4-inch of edge. Place jalapeño slices and sliced shrimp on top.

4. Bake 6 to 8 minutes or until cheeses are melted and the tortillas start to brown slightly. Remove from oven and fold in half. Cut each half into three pieces.

5. Place pieces on serving plates. Garnish each piece with a dollop of sour cream. Arrange tomatoes over cream and avocado. Sprinkle with paprika.

Makes 4 servings.

STUFFED JALAPEÑO CHILE PEPPERS

If you can find the red-ripe jalapeño chiles you are in for a treat. The mature pepper has a rich warm flavor. I fix these stuffed jewels as often as I can.

18	*ripe red jalapeño chiles*
1	*(8-oz.) pkg. cream cheese, softened*
2	*tablespoons lime juice*
1	*teaspoon ground cumin*
1	*teaspoon ground red New Mexico chile*
	dash fresh ground black pepper
2	*tablespoons vegetable oil*
1/2	*cup chopped pecans*
1/2	*small white onion chopped*
	Cilantro, finely chopped

1. Cut jalapeños in half lengthwise. Remove seeds and devein. Set aside.

2. In a medium bowl, combine all ingredients except pecans, onions and cilantro. Beat with electric mixer until smooth.

3. Stir in pecans and onions. Stuff jalapeños with cream cheese till slightly rounded. Cover and refrigerate at least 8 hours. Serve sprinkled with cilantro.

Makes 36 stuffed chiles.

The next time you have a party, prepare a full platter of these little red treats. A wonderful way to present the mature version of our most popular chile pepper.

SPICY CHEESE STICKS

These hors d'oeuvres are winners. Your guests will want more than one.

1 1/2	*cups sifted all-purpose flour*
1	*tablespoon baking powder*
3/4	*teaspoon salt (optional)*
1/8	*to 1/4 teaspoon cayenne chile powder, or to taste*
1/3	*cup vegetable shortening, chilled*
1	*cup shredded Cheddar cheese*
3	*tablespoons white onion, minced*
1	*tablespoon Worcestershire sauce*
1	*teaspoon Tabasco Sauce*
2/3	*cup buttermilk*
2	*tablespoons butter, melted*
1/4	*cup freshly grated Parmesan cheese*

1. Sift together the flour, baking powder, salt, and cayenne chile into a medium mixing bowl.

2. Add shortening and cut in with a pastry blender until well incorporated. Stir in Cheddar cheese, onion and Worcestershire and Tabasco sauces.

3. Add buttermilk and stir to make a soft dough. Wrap in waxed paper or plastic wrap and chill for 1 hour.

4. Preheat oven to 475F(375C).

5. On a lightly floured board, roll out dough into an 8-x-12-inch rectangle. Wrap loosely around rolling pin and transfer to a cold lightly greased baking sheet.

6. With a metal spatula, cut dough in half lengthwise, then cut across at 1-inch intervals to form sticks. Brush sticks with melted butter, sprinkle with Parmesan, and bake until lightly browned, about 10 minutes. Immediately remove from baking sheet and serve hot, or cool on wire racks before storing in airtight containers.

Makes 24 sticks.

SALADS
and SOUPS

For years I have looked for a potato salad with New Mexican flair. Recently, I found a great one–Peppery Potato Salad–and I want to share it with you. This is a colorful, tasty creation that you will prepare again and again. It is easy to fix and can be prepared ahead of time. This one is a sure hit. For a different salad why not try Taos Black-Eyed-Pea salad. The combination of jicama, red bell peppers, zucchini and black-eyed peas is not only great eating, but makes a beautiful presentation. It looks as good as it tastes.

With soups, some like them hot and some like them cool. I present both, easy to prepare and sure to please. For a cool treat, the Santa Fe Gazpacho is a refreshingly cold, summertime soup; or try Chilled Squash Soup, low in fat and yet full and rich-tasting. If it is hot you want, the Green Chile Stew or Meatball Soup with Vegetables are sure to warm you on a cold night. Both of these dishes are old standards here in the Land of Enchantment.

JALAPEÑO PASTA SALAD

An attractive salad low in fat and easy to fix. It tastes as good as it looks.

1-1/3	**cups bow-tie pasta (farfalle)**
1/2	**cup nonfat yogurt**
1	**tablespoon Dijon mustard**
1/2	**teaspoon salt**
3	**Roma tomatoes, cut lengthwise in half and sliced**
2	**green onions, cut diagonally into 1/2-inch pieces**
2	**jalapeño chiles seeded and finely minced**
1	**large garlic clove. minced**
	lettuce leaves

1. Cook pasta as directed on package; drain. Rinse with cold water; drain.

2. In large bowl mix pasta and remaining ingredients except lettuce. Cover and refrigerate until chilled. Serve on lettuce leaves.

Makes 6 servings.

If your luck is running out at the horse track in Ruidoso, try the Deming, New Mexico, Great American Duck Races held each year in late August. Besides fast feathered quacky races, you will find dancing and hot-air balloon races. There is also a tortilla toss, a craft show and flea market.

JICAMA SALAD

The nutty, slightly sweet taste and crisp texture of the jicama are complemented with citrus fruits, creating a fresh light flavor.

2   *medium jicamas*
2   *oranges*
2   *limes*
1 /4   *cup golden raisins*
1   *tablespoon sunflower seeds, chopped*
1/4   *teaspoon salt*
2   *teaspoons mint leaves, chopped*
    lettuce leaves
    dash of chili powder

Dressing:
liquid from salad
1   *tablespoon vegetable oil*
2   *tablespoons plain nonfat yogurt*

1. Using a sharp knife, remove thick outer brown peel of jicama. Cut into bite size pieces, making about 2 cups.

2. Peel oranges and remove seeds and membranes. Slice into thin slices. Juice limes.

3. In a bowl, combine the jicama, orange slices, 1/2 of lime juice, raisins, sunflower seeds, salt and mint leaves. Refrigerate for several hours.

4. Remove from refrigerator and bring to cool room temperature. Drain excess liquid into small bowl; add dressing ingredients stir well. Pour over salad and toss to coat.

5. Serve on bed of leaf lettuce. Sprinkle with a dash of chili powder.

Makes 6 servings.

PEPPERY POTATO SALAD

This is the one for your Fourth of July celebration. It travels well and it is a crowd pleaser.

>   3   *lbs. red potatoes, peeled and cut into 1/2 inch-thick slices*
>   2   *tablespoons white wine-vinegar*
>   1   *yellow bell pepper, seeded and cut into 1-1/2 inch julienne strips*
>   1   *red bell pepper, seeded and cut into 1-1/2 inch julienne strips*
>   3   *New Mexican peppers, roasted, peeled, seeded and cut into 1-1/2 inch julienne strips*
>   1/2   *cup minced green onions with tops*
>   1/3   *cup fresh parsley, minced*
>   1   *tablespoon drained capers*
>   1   *Hot Salsa Mayonnaise dressing*
>   *Lettuce leaves*
>   *Tomato wedges*

1. Cut potato slices in half, and place in a 3-quart saucepan. Cover with water, and bring to a boil. Boil 4 to 5 minutes or until tender. Drain immediately, and transfer to a large bowl.

2. Sprinkle potatoes with vinegar, and toss to coat.

3. Add peppers, green onions, parsley, capers, and Hot Salsa Mayonnaise Dressing to potatoes; stir well. Cover and chill thoroughly. Serve on lettuce leaves. Garnish with tomato wedges.

Hot Salsa Mayonnaise Dressing

>   2   *cloves garlic, crushed*
>   1/4   *cup reduced-calorie mayonnaise*
>   1/3   *cup commercial hot salsa*
>   1   *tablespoon sweet pickle relish*

1. Combine all ingredients in a small bowl; mix well. Cover and refrigerate 1 hour or until thoroughly chilled.

Makes 8 servings.

TAOS BLACK-EYED PEA SALAD

Attractive, colorful, tasty, what more could you want in a salad.

1	*medium jicama*
2	*cups water*
2	*(10-oz.) packages frozen black-eyed peas*
1/4	*cup chopped fresh cilantro*
1	*medium zucchini*
1	*red bell pepper coarsely chopped*

Dressing:

1/3	*cup lemon juice*
1	*teaspoon sugar*
1/2	*teaspoon chili powder*
1/2	*teaspoon cumin*
1/8	*teaspoon ground red New Mexico chile*
1/2	*teaspoon garlic clove, minced*
2	*teaspoons vegetable oil*
6	*lettuce leaves*

1. Using sharp knife, remove brown peel of jicama. Rinse and cut into 1-1/2 x 1/4-inch sticks. Peel and cut zucchini into 1-1/2 x 1/4-inch sticks. Set aside.

2. In a 2-quart saucepan bring water to a boil; add black-eyed peas. Bring water to full boil; reduce heat to low. Cover; cook 18-22 minutes until black-eyed peas are tender. Drain; rinse with cold water. Cool 5 minutes.

3. In a large bowl, combine black-eyed peas and remaining salad ingredients.

4. In a small bowl, whisk together all dressing ingredients except lettuce. Pour over salad and toss well. Serve warm or chilled on lettuce leaves.

Makes 6 servings.

Sassy Southwest Cooking

TOSTADO SALAD

A refreshing salad that is a complete meal in itself. I like the contrast of the cold shredded lettuce, warm filling and melted cheese.

6	*(8-inch) flour tortillas*
3	*tablespoons butter, melted*
1	*lb. lean ground beef*
1	*teaspoon ground red New Mexico chile*
1/4	*teaspoon ground cumin*
1/4	*teaspoon dried-leaf oregano*
1/4	*teaspoon garlic powder*
1/4	*teaspoon onion powder*
1/8	*teaspoon freshly ground black pepper*
1/2	*cup tomato sauce*
1/2	*cup water*
2	*cups shredded lettuce*
1	*(15.5-oz.) can kidney beans, drained*
1	*large tomato, seeded, chopped*
1	*small white onion, chopped*
1/2	*cup ripe black olives, sliced*
1/2	*cup avocado, peeled, seeded and diced*
1	*(8-oz.) jar of jalapeño flavor pasteurized processed cheese spread, melted*
	Dairy sour cream

1. Preheat oven to 350F(175C). Lightly brush melted butter on each side of tortillas. Place tortillas on cookie sheets. Bake 10 to 12 minutes or until dry, crisp and lightly browned. Set aside.

2. In a large skillet, brown ground beef; drain. Add seasonings, tomato sauce and water; simmer for 5 minutes, stirring occasionally.

3. To assemble, place baked tortillas on serving plates; top each with lettuce, beans, tomato, onion, olives and avocado. Pour melted cheese over salad. Serve with sour cream.

Makes 6 servings.

WEST OF THE PECOS PASTA SALAD

Colorful and tasty, this is a great use of tomatillos.

1	*(20-oz) can pineapple chunks*
6	*fresh tomatillos*
3	*cups tricolor pasta spirals*
1/2	*jalapeño chile, seeded and chopped*
2	*tablespoons canola oil*
1	*tablespoon fresh cilantro, chopped*
1/2	*teaspoon grated lime peel*
1/4	*teaspoon salt*

1. Drain pineapple, reserve 2 tablespoons of juice.

2. Remove husks from fresh tomatillos and cut into 8 wedges.

3. Cook pasta as directed on package; drain and rinse with cold water and drain.

4. In a serving bowl, mix pasta, tomatillos, chile and pineapple.

5. In a small bowl, mix reserved pineapple juice and remaining ingredients. Pour over pasta mixture; toss. Cover and refrigerate at least 2 hours until chilled.

Makes 6 servings.

Tomatillos are fat little vegetables slightly larger than cherry tomatoes. They grow in papery husks reminiscent of Japanese lanterns and taste best when they are brilliant green in color. By the time they begin to turn yellow, they have lost some of their acid freshness. Select tomatillos with their husks still drawn tightly around them. Husk and rinse off the sticky residue before using them.

BLACK BEAN CHICKEN SOUP

Black beans are now readily available, and you will find them an interesting treat in this unusual soup.

1	*tablespoon olive oil*
1	*large onion, chopped*
1	*clove garlic, chopped*
2	*(14-oz.) cans chicken broth*
1	*(14- or 15-oz.) can black beans, rinsed and drained*
2	*(4-oz.) cans green chile peppers, chopped, undrained*
2	*teaspoons dried-leaf oregano, crushed*
1-1/2	*teaspoons ground cumin*
1	*teaspoon garlic powder*
1/4	*teaspoon ground cloves*
1/4	*teaspoon ground red chile*
3	*cups cooked chicken, diced*
	Lowfat cheddar cheese, shredded (optional)

1. In a 4-quart Dutch oven or heavy pot, heat olive oil; add onion and garlic; cook until soft.

2. Add remaining ingredients, except for chicken and cheese.

3. Bring to a boil and reduce heat, cover and simmer for 20 minutes, stirring occasionally.

4. Add chicken; cook covered, about 10 minutes or until heated through.

5. If desired, serve with cheese sprinkled on top.

Makes 4 servings.

CHILLED SQUASH SOUP

This cool and colorful soup is a good example of a snappy taste. The jalapeño pepper lends a delightful contrast to the mild squash.

2	*tablespoons margarine*
2	*garlic cloves, minced*
1	*medium onion, chopped*
1	*jalapeño chile, cut into rings and seeded*
2	*teaspoons sugar*
1-1/2	*teaspoons curry powder*
1/2	*teaspoon dry mustard*
1/4	*teaspoon ground allspice*
4	*cups water*
1-1/2	*teaspoons chicken-flavored bullion granules*
1/3	*cup uncooked regular rice*
4	*medium yellow squash, sliced*
1	*(8-oz.) carton plain nonfat yogurt*
2	*tablespoons fresh lime juice*
1/4	*cup green onions, minced*

1. In a 6-quart saucepan, melt margarine, add garlic, and saute 1 minute or until tender.

2. Add onion and jalapeño pepper; stir well. Add sugar, curry powder, mustard, allspice. Cook 4 to 5 minutes over medium heat, stirring constantly.

3. Add water, bullion granules, rice, and sliced yellow squash to vegetable mixture and bring to boil. Cover, reduce heat and simmer 20 to 30 minutes or until rice is tender.

4. In a blender or food processor, blend 1/2 of the cooked mixture. Repeat process with remaining mixture.

5. Pour into a large bowl. Cover and refrigerate 12 hours or overnight.

6. To serve, stir yogurt and lime juice into chilled soup. Top with minced green onions.

Makes 6-8 Servings.

Sassy Southwest Cooking

GREEN CHILE STEW

Traditional in many homes. It is one of the first truly
New Mexican dishes I learned to make.

2	*lbs. boneless pork, cut into 1-inch cubes*
3	*tablespoons all-purpose flour*
2	*tablespoons butter*
1	*cup white onion, chopped*
2	*garlic cloves, minced*
3	*cups ripe tomatoes, peeled, chopped*
1	*teaspoon salt*
1/2	*teaspoon dried-leaf oregano*
1/4	*teaspoon ground cumin*
20	*fresh New Mexico chiles, roasted, peeled, seeded, deveined and chopped*

1. Toss pork with flour, to coat. In a 4-quart Dutch
   oven or heavy pot, heat butter and add pork cubes a
   few at a time. Stir to brown. Push to side of pot and
   add onion, garlic and cook until onion is soft. Stir in
   browned pork.

2. Add tomatoes, salt, oregano and cumin. Cover and
   simmer 1 hour, add water as necessary and stir
   occasionally. Add chiles, simmer 30 minutes and add
   water as necessary.

Makes 4 servings.

HOPI LAMB STEW

Still used today this old stew recipe is a nice way to enjoy lamb. Sheep production is still very important to the Hopi Indians. I learned how to make this stew from a sheepherder in the early 1960's.

4	*lbs. lamb shoulder, bone in*
6	*quarts water*
1	*white onion, quartered*
2	*garlic cloves, chopped*
6	*juniper berries, crushed*
1	*teaspoon salt*
1/2	*teaspoon black peppercorns*
1/2	*teaspoon dried-sage leaves*
1	*(26-oz.) can hominy, rinsed and drained*
1/2	*cup onion, finely chopped for garnish*
1	*(4-oz.) can green chile finely chopped for garnish*

1. Trim fat and connective tissue from lamb shoulder. Place in large stock pot and cover with 4 inches of cold water.

2. Bring to boil; lower heat to medium. Skim as needed. Add water as needed to keep water level 3 inches above meat. Simmer for 1 hour.

3. Add onion, garlic, juniper berries, salt, peppercorns and sage to pot. Simmer 1 hour longer, skimming if needed.

4. Strain broth through cloth lined colander into another pot. Remove vegetables, herbs and spices and return meat to strained broth. Add hominy and simmer, covered for 30 minutes. Serve hot with onions and chile as garnish.

Makes 6 servings.

Sassy Southwest Cooking

MEATBALL SOUP WITH VEGETABLES

I first tasted this soup when we moved here. It is a New Mexico dish that is little known outside this state.

Meatballs:

1/2	*pound chuck steak cut into small pieces*
1/2	*pound pork shoulder, cut into small pieces*
2/3	*cup dry bread crumbs*
1	*egg*
1/3	*cup milk*
1	*teaspoon salt*
1	*teaspoon ground coriander*
1	*teaspoon dried-leaf oregano, crushed*
1/4	*teaspoon fresh ground black pepper*
1/4	*cup canned green chiles, chopped*
1/4	*medium white onion, coarsely chopped*
2	*garlic cloves, chopped*
1	*dried chipotle chile, stemmed, seeded and crumbled*

Broth and vegetables:

2	*cups beef broth*
2	*cups chicken broth*
1/2	*cup each of turnips, zucchini, peeled carrots, all cut into thin 2-inch strips*
1/4	*cup fresh cilantro, chopped*

1. In a food processor or blender process meat until coarse ground.

2. In a bowl, combine bread crumbs, egg and milk and stir with fork to moisten the crumbs. Add to the meat along with the remaining ingredients. Process until the mixture is smooth.

3. Shape mixture into small meatballs. Use 1 tablespoon for each ball. Set aside.

4. In a 4-quart saucepan combine broth and bring to a boil. Drop in meat balls, cook for 5 minutes. Add vegetables, cover and simmer for 10 minutes. Serve immediately, garnish with cilantro.

Makes 6 servings.

SANTA FE GAZPACHO

Santa Fe has numerous outdoor restaurants, and this is a popular mid-day lunch in this enchanting city. I also like it served with sourdough bread.

1	*white onion diced*
3	*garlic cloves, minced*
1/2	*teaspoon salt*
1	*tablespoon extra virgin olive oil*
5	*cups vegetables stock, divided*
9	*ripe tomatoes, cored*
1	*cucumber, trimmed and peeled*
5	*ripe tomatoes, finely diced*
1	*jalapeño chile, seeded and diced*
2	*New Mexico green chiles, roasted, seeded, deveined and diced*
1	*red bell pepper, seeded and diced*
2	*tablespoons minced parsley*
2	*tablespoons minced cilantro*
1/4	*cup lemon juice*
2	*tablespoons lime juice*
	salt and fresh ground black pepper to taste
16	*or more romaine lettuce leaves*
16	*Slices dry French bread, broken up*

1. In a medium skillet heat olive oil, add onion and garlic and cook until onions are soft. Transfer to blender and add salt and 3 cups vegetable stock, blend until smooth. Pour into large bowl.

2. In blender, place tomatoes, cucumber and 2 cups of stock and blend. May be done in two batches. Add mixture to onion stock mixture in large bowl. Add remaining minced vegetables, herbs and juices to soup. Season to taste with salt and freshly ground black pepper.

3. Cover and refrigerate 1 hour before serving. To serve line deep bowls or stemmed glasses with lettuce leaves. Add soup and bread in layers and serve with long handled spoons.

Makes 6 to 8 servings.

BREADS

I love the taste and smell of fresh baked goods. I remember the aroma of my Aunt Tiny's baked bread, fresh from her old wood-burning stove. It's been many years since I last sat down at her table for a lunch of oven-warm Pecan Biscuits, hand churned-butter, sweet onions and cold fresh milk.

I present a varied and palate-pleasing assortment of breads, biscuits and muffins. Some are new, such as Green Chile Muffins and Ranch Buttermilk-Bran Muffins. All are recipes that are sure to please.

I realize that it is easier to go to the supermarket and take coffeecake or bread off the shelf, but that special smell and taste of homemade baked goods cannot be matched by any commercially baked breads or pastries.

GREEN CHILE MUFFINS

These are moist and do not crumble. They go well with all New Mexican meals. Try the different corn meals for variety.

3/4	*cup milk*
1	*(8-oz.) can cream-style corn*
1/3	*cup melted butter, or vegetable oil*
2	*eggs beaten*
1-1/2	*cups white, yellow or blue cornmeal*
1	*teaspoon baking powder*
1/2	*teaspoon baking soda*
1	*teaspoon salt*
1	*teaspoon sugar*
1-1/2	*cups mixed shredded Cheddar cheese and Monterey Jack cheese*
1	*(4-oz.) can chopped New Mexico chiles, drained*

1. Preheat oven to 400F(205C). Line 18 muffin cups with paper liners or grease and flour each cup.

2. In a medium-size bowl, stir together milk, corn, butter, and eggs.

3. In a large bowl, whisk together cornmeal, baking powder, baking soda, salt, and sugar. Add mixture from medium-size bowl to dry ingredients and mix just until combined. Do not over mix.

4. Spoon a large spoonful of batter into each prepared muffin cup and top with a little cheese mixture and green chile, dividing evenly and reserving a little for sprinkling on top. Top with remaining batter and reserved cheese and green chile. Each cup should be two-thirds full.

5. Bake 25 to 30 minutes, or until muffins are golden and a wooden pick inserted into the center comes out clean.

Makes 18 muffins.

HOPI PIKI BREAD

Another ceremonial bread of the American Indian. Wafer thin and delicate, it takes quite a bit of practice to get this one right.

1/4	**cup blue corn masa or cornmeal, fine ground**
3/4	**teaspoon salt**
7	**cups water**
1/4	**cup cornstarch mixed with 1 cup cold water**
2	**tablespoons vegetable shortening**

1. In a 3-quart saucepan, combine masa and salt, slowly stir in water. When well mixed, bring to a boil, stirring constantly. Reduce heat, simmer 15 minutes, stirring occasionally.

2. Stir cornstarch and add to masa mixture. Bring to a boil and cook for 2 minutes, stirring constantly.

3. Heat an electric griddle to 350F(175C) or a cast-iron griddle over medium heat until a drop of water dances on the surface. Coat the griddle with shortening; when hot, add the batter 1/3 to 1/2 cup at a time. Take care the batter does not splatter on you. Once the mixture is on the griddle, spread it with a spatula to form a rectangle. Bake until dry, about 4 to 5 minutes.

Makes 6 to 8 pieces.

In a solemn ritual, with precise movements, Hopi Indians use blue corn meal to make Piki bread. Three sheets of this paper thin bread rolled together into a scroll make one piki. The piki is used by the Hopi girl when she decides to propose to a boy. She does so by leaving a large plate of bread on his door step. If he takes the bread into his home, he accepts her marriage proposal.

PEANUT HONEY COFFEE CAKE

Quick and easy, but with a great taste, you must try this cake. Of all my coffee cake recipes none are easier to make or better eating.

>   2   *cups packaged biscuit mix*
>   2   *tablespoons sugar*
>   1   *egg, slightly beaten*
>   2/3   *cup milk*
>   1/4   *cup honey*
>   1/4   *cup creamy peanut butter*

Topping:
>   1/2   *cup packed brown sugar*
>   1/2   *cup packaged biscuit mix*
>   1/4   *cup chopped peanuts*
>   2   *tablespoons butter*
>   2   *tablespoons creamy peanut butter*
>   1/2   *teaspoon ground cinnamon*

1. Grease a 9 x 9 x 2-inch baking pan. Preheat oven to 400F(205C).

2. In a medium bowl combine biscuit mix and sugar. Add egg and milk. Blend in honey and the peanut butter. The mixture will be lumpy.

2. Turn into prepared pan.

3. Combine topping ingredients until crumbly; sprinkle over batter. Bake for 20 to 25 minutes. Cool and cut into squares.

Makes 6 servings.

PECAN BISCUITS

A bed-and-breakfast specialty, this is an excellent way to start your day. There is nothing like the smell of biscuits in the morning. The cinnamon and sugar make a nice topping.

1-3/4	*cups all-purpose flour*
3	*tablespoons sugar*
2	*teaspoons baking powder*
1/2	*teaspoon salt*
1/4	*cup shortening*
1	*egg beaten*
3/4	*cup milk*
1/3	*cup pecans, chopped finely*

Topping:
2	*tablespoons sugar*
1/2	*teaspoon ground cinnamon*

1. Preheat oven to 425F(220C).

2. In a medium size mixing bowl, combine flour, sugar, baking powder and salt. Cut in shortening until mixture has appearance of coarse crumbs.

3. In a small bowl, combine beaten egg and milk; add all at once to dry mixture, stirring just until dough clings together. Stir in pecans.

4. Drop by heaping teaspoons onto a greased baking sheet. For topping, combine sugar and cinnamon; sprinkle over biscuits. Bake for 8 to 10 minutes.

Makes 36 biscuits.

PECAN & CRANBERRY BRAN MUFFINS

I love muffins, so I am always on the look-out for unusual recipes and found this one in a little cafe in Las Cruces. It has a full rich flavor and nice texture.

1	*cup oat bran*
1/2	*cup corn meal*
2/3	*cup all-purpose flour*
2-1/2	*teaspoons baking powder*
1/2	*teaspoon salt*
2	*teaspoons non-fat dry milk*
1/4	*cup pecans, chopped*
1/4	*cup raisins*
3	*egg whites*
2	*teaspoons vegetable oil*
3/4	*cup skim milk*
1/3	*cup honey*
1	*teaspoon vanilla extract*
1	*cup fresh cranberries, halved*

1. Preheat oven to 400F(205C). Spray muffin pan with vegetable cooking spray or paper line muffin cups.

2. In a large bowl, combine bran, cornmeal, flour, baking powder, salt, dry-milk powder, pecans and raisins; set aside.

3. In a medium bowl, beat egg whites with oil. Add skim milk, honey, vanilla and cranberries.

4. Combine dry and wet ingredients, stir only to moisten, batter will be lumpy. Spoon into prepared muffin pan. Bake 20 to 25 minutes or until a wooden pick inserted into center comes out clean, remove from pan; cool 5 minutes and serve.

Makes 12 muffins.

RANCH BUTTERMILK-BRAN MUFFINS

Here is a stick-to-your-ribs version of muffins, a sure winner. Healthful and hearty they freeze well but are best when served hot from the oven.

1	cup buttermilk
1-1/2	cup whole bran cereal
1/2	cup sugar
1/3	cup shortening
1	egg
1-1/2	cups all-purpose flour
2	teaspoons baking powder
1/2	teaspoon baking soda
1/2	teaspoon salt

1. Preheat oven to 400F(205C). Spray a muffin pan with vegetable cooking spray.

2. In a bowl, stir together buttermilk and bran; let stand until liquid is absorbed.

3. In another bowl, thoroughly cream shortening and egg. Combine remaining ingredients and buttermilk-bran mixture.

5. Spoon batter into prepared muffin pan. Bake 25 minutes or until a wooden pick inserted into center comes out clean, remove from pan; cool 5 minutes and serve.

Makes 12 muffins.

SPICED PUMPKIN BREAD

Every year around Halloween time, my wife makes this bread and I can hardly wait for it to cool. The second loaf keeps well for 6 weeks if you wrap it in foil and freeze it.

1	*cup vegetable oil*
3	*cups sugar*
3	*large eggs*
1	*(16-oz) can solid pack pumpkin*
3	*cups all purpose flour*
1	*teaspoon cinnamon*
1	*teaspoon nutmeg*
1	*teaspoon ground cloves*
1	*teaspoon baking soda*
1/2	*teaspoon salt*
1/2	*teaspoon baking powder*
1	*cup coarsely chopped pecans*

1. Preheat oven to 350F(175C). Butter and flour two loaf pans.

2. In a large bowl, beat oil, sugar to blend. Mix in eggs and pumpkin.

3. In a second large bowl, Sift flour, cinnamon, nutmeg, cloves, baking soda, salt and baking powder. Stir into pumpkin mixture in two additions. Mix in pecans.

4. Divide batter equally between prepared loaf pans. Bake until wooden pick inserted into center comes out clean. About one hour and 10 minutes. Transfer pans to wire rack and cool for 10 minutes. Turn out bread onto racks by cutting along edges to loosen. Cool completely.

Makes 2 loaves.

MAIN DISHES

Who says you can't have sassy food that is lowfat? Here are a number of main dishes that offer taste, texture and color. From new versions of some of the old standards like Chimichangas and Burritos, to new ones like Green Chile Cheeseburgers, comes the full rich flavor of New Mexico's exciting food.

I have included my wife Millie's Brisket and a new treat called Four Beans and a Pea Cassoulet, a sure fire meal in a crockpot. Prepared from readily available canned goods, here's one you mix together and put in a crockpot, and leave for the day. When you come home you have a wonderful meal fit for a king.

Light 'N Fancy Tostado cups give you a chance to show off. This delicacy can even make folks refer to you as a Chef, yet it is simple and easy to put together.

BAKED CHIMICHANGAS

Here is a different method of preparing a traditionally fried dish.

1	*lb. lean ground beef*
1/4	*cup onion, finely chopped*
1	*tablespoon red wine vinegar*
1	*teaspoon ground red chiles*
1/4	*teaspoon ground cinnamon*
1/8	*teaspoon ground cloves*
1	*(4-oz.) can New Mexico green chile, chopped*
1	*medium tomato, chopped*
8	*(10-inch) flour tortillas*
1	*egg, beaten*
2	*tablespoons butter or margarine, softened* *salsa*

1. In 10-inch skillet, cook beef and onion, stirring occasionally until beef is browned; drain.

2. Stir in vinegar, ground red chiles, cinnamon, cloves, green chiles and tomato. Bring to boil, reduce heat. Simmer uncovered for 20 minutes.

3. Warm tortillas by placing in a 250F(125C) oven for 15 minutes or wrap in dampened microwavable paper towels and microwave on high for 15 to 20 seconds.

4. Spoon 1/8 of the beef mixture onto the center of each tortilla and brush edges with beaten egg mixture fold envelope style to seal. Brush each chimichanga with butter or margarine and place seam side down on a large ungreased baking sheet.

5. Preheat oven to 500F(260C). Bake uncovered for 8 to 10 minutes or until tortillas begin to brown and filling is hot. Serve with salsa.

Makes 8 servings.

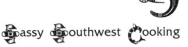

BEEF BURRITOS

To satisfy a hearty appetite, try this old favorite. There is nothing like a beef burrito.

2	*cups New Mexican Meat Filling (page 76)*
1	*cup or 1 (15.5-oz.) can refried beans*
8	*(10-inch) flour tortillas*
2	*cups shredded lettuce*
1	*cup shredded Cheddar cheese*
1/2	*cup dairy sour cream*
1/4	*cup tomatoes, chopped*

1. In a small skillet, heat New Mexican Meat Mix.

2. Warm tortillas by placing in a 250F(125C) oven for 15 minutes or by wrapping several in dampened microwavable towel and microwave on high for 15 to 20 seconds.

3. Spoon 1/4 cup of meat mix onto center of each tortilla. Spoon 2 tablespoons of beans onto beef mixture. Top with lettuce, tomatoes, sour cream and cheese.

4. Fold filled tortillas envelope style.

Makes 8 burritos.

CHICKEN BURRITOS WITH BLACK BEANS AND PAPAYA

Papaya gives these burritos a sweetness that, when combined with the heat of the chile, presents the ultimate in sassy taste.

4	*chicken breast halves, boned and skinned*
1	*(14.5-oz.) can chicken broth*
1	*bay leaf*
1/2	*teaspoon ground cumin*
1/2	*cup white onion, chopped*
1	*tablespoon oil of choice*
1	*(16-oz.) can black beans, drained and rinsed*
2	*jalapeño peppers, seeded and finely chopped*
8	*(10-inch) flour tortillas*
1	*ripe papaya, seeded, peeled and thinly sliced*
1	*cup shredded Monterey Jack cheese*
1/4	*cup fresh cilantro, snipped*
	salsa

1. In a skillet, place chicken breasts, chicken broth, bay leaf and cumin. Bring to boil; reduce heat cover and simmer for 15 to 20 minutes or until chicken is tender and no longer pink. Remove bay leaf.

2. Drain and reserve 1/4 cup of broth. Let chicken stand until cool.

3. Heat oil in large skillet, cook onion until soft but not brown. Add beans, jalapeño peppers, and reserved 1/4 cup of broth.

4. Preheat oven to 350F(175C). Mash beans. Meanwhile, stack tortillas and wrap tightly in foil. Heat in preheated oven 2 minutes to soften.

(Continued on next page)

CHICKEN BURRITOS WITH BLACK BEANS AND PAPAYA

(Continued from preceding page)

5. Spread about 3 tablespoons bean mixture down the middle of each tortilla.

6. Using a fork, pull chicken into long thin threads.

7. Top each tortilla with shredded chicken, papaya, shredded cheese and cilantro.

8. Fold filled tortillas envelope style and secure with toothpick.

9. Place burritos on a baking sheet. Cover loosely with foil. Place in oven and bake until heated thoroughly. Serve with salsa.

Makes 4 to 6 servings.

BROILED CHICKEN WITH TOMATO RAISIN SAUCE

Full of flavor, this chicken is enhanced by a tangy raisin sauce.

3   *tablespoons fresh cilantro, minced*
6   *garlic cloves, minced divided*
2   *teaspoons fresh ground black pepper*
1   *pound skinless chicken white or brown meat, cut into 1-1/2-inch pieces.*
1/3   *cup tomato sauce*
1   *tablespoon packed brown sugar*
1   *tablespoon cider vinegar*
1/2   *cup raisins*

1. Preheat oven to 450F(230C).

2. In a small bowl, mix cilantro, 4 garlic cloves, and black pepper. Rub mixture over chicken. Place chicken pieces well apart on lightly oiled 10x15-inch baking pan.

3. Bake 20 to 25 minutes until lightly browned and no longer pink in center.

4. In a food processor or blender, blend remaining 2 cloves garlic, tomato sauce, brown sugar, vinegar, and raisins until raisins are chopped.

5. Serve chicken hot with tomato raisin sauce.

Makes 4 servings.

 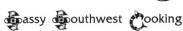

CARNE ASADA (Grilled Steak)

Lime juice and spices enhance the steak, grilling adds the final touch.

1/4	*cup olive oil*
6	*garlic cloves*
2	*tablespoons lime juice*
2	*teaspoons dried-leaf rosemary*
1/2	*teaspoon ground red New Mexico chile*
1/2	*teaspoon dried-leaf oregano*
1/4	*teaspoon ground cumin*
2	*lbs. beef flank steak*
3	*medium white onions, cut into 1/2-inch slices*
	warmed flour or corn tortillas
	salsa
	Guacamole, (page 26)

1. In a blender or food processor, puree olive oil, garlic, lime juice, rosemary, ground chile, oregano and cumin.

2. Rub garlic-herb paste on both sides of steak.

3. Broil steaks 4 inches from heat source for 6 to 8 minutes, per side.

4. In small skillet heat oil; cook onions until soft. Or, grill steaks and onion slices over medium coals until meat is medium rare, 12 to 15 minutes. Turn once. Onions should be tender in 15 to 18 minutes.

5. Thinly slice steak across grain. Serve wrapped in warm tortillas with salsa and Guacamole (page 26).

Makes 4 to 6 servings.

CHALUPAS

Hot and spicy, great company fare. This festive traditional dish is a fine example of the full rich taste of New Mexican cooking.

2	*lbs. lean pork, cubed*
4	*tablespoons vegetable oil, divided*
2	*tablespoons all-purpose flour*
1	*cup water*
1	*teaspoon ground cumin*
	garlic salt to taste
1	*(14-oz.) can tomatoes, chopped*
4	*(4-oz.) cans green chiles, chopped*
8	*corn tortillas*
2	*whole chicken breasts*
2	*(7-oz.) cans chicken broth*
3	*cups Refried Beans (page 92)*
2	*cups Guacamole (page 26)*
1-1/2	*cups grated Cheddar cheese (6-oz.)*
1	*cup dairy sour cream (8-oz.)*

1. In a 10-inch skillet, heat 3 tablespoons vegetable oil and fry corn tortillas one at a time until crisp. Drain on paper towels, set aside.

2. In large Dutch oven or heavy pot, heat 1 tablespoon vegetable oil; brown pork; stir in flour, add water, cumin, garlic salt, tomatoes and green chiles. Simmer until thick, stirring occasionally.

3. In saucepan, simmer chicken breasts in chicken broth 15 minutes. Remove from broth and shred. Set aside.

4. To assemble, begin with tortilla; top with layer of refried beans, pork in sauce, shredded chicken, guacamole, cheese and sour cream.

Makes 8 servings.

NEW MEXICO STYLE VEAL PARMESAN

Here is a new way to prepare an old standard. Another example of the ever-changing cuisine of this Land of Enchantment.

1/2	*cup canned refried beans*
1/2	*cup Tomato Salsa (page 148)*
6	*corn tortillas (6 or 7-inch)*
2	*teaspoons vegetable oil*
2	*cups cooked chicken, cut up into small pieces*
3/4	*cup shredded Monterey Jack cheese*
3	*cups shredded lettuce*
1	*avocado, peeled, pitted and cut into 12 slices*
	sour cream

1. In small skillets, heat salsa and beans separately.

2. In another 10-inch skillet, heat oil and cook tortillas, one at a time for 1 minute or until crisp; drain on paper towel.

3. Spread each tortilla with 1/4 cup of Beans. Top with 2 tablespoons of chicken and 2 more tablespoons of salsa. Sprinkle each with 2 tablespoons of cheese.

4. Set oven control to broil. Place tortillas on rack in broiler pan. Broil with tops 2 to 3 inches from heat 3 minutes or until cheese melts. Top each with 1/2 cup of shredded lettuce, 2 avocado slices and sour cream. Serve immediately.

Makes 6 servings.

CORN CHOWDER CON QUESO

Enjoy a hearty, vegetarian meal in one dish. I serve this with sourdough bread and a simple green salad.

1	*tablespoon butter or oil*
2	*medium white onions, chopped*
3/4	*cup celery, chopped*
3	*cups frozen whole kernel corn, thawed*
1	*large unpeeled potato, finely chopped*
1	*red bell pepper, chopped*
1	*(14.5-oz.) can low salt chicken broth*
1	*(14.5-oz.) can diced tomatoes*
2	*jalapeño chiles, seeded and finely chopped*
1	*tablespoon chili powder*
1/2	*teaspoon salt*
1/4	*teaspoon ground cumin*
1	*cup skim milk*
2	*tablespoons cornstarch*
2	*tablespoons chopped fresh cilantro*
4	*oz. shredded Monterey Jack cheese*

1. In a large Dutch oven or heavy pot, heat butter or oil to sizzling and add onions and celery. Cook until soft.

2. Stir in corn, potato, bell pepper, broth, tomatoes, jalapeño peppers, chili powder, salt and ground cumin. Over medium heat, bring to a full boil, reduce heat. Cover; cook 15 to 18 minutes until potatoes are fork tender.

3. In a small bowl, stir 2 tablespoons of milk into cornstarch until smooth. Stir in remaining milk; stir mixture into soup. Cook 3 to 4 minutes over medium high heat until mixture comes to a full boil.

4. Reduce heat to low. Cook, stirring occasionally, 5 minutes. Stir in cilantro. Serve topped with cheese.

Makes 8 servings.

DE BACA LAMB STEW

The Emillio de Baca family shared this dish with me and it is the only way I like lamb. A special dish from a special family.

1/4	*cup oil*
1	*medium white onion, diced*
3	*garlic cloves, minced*
1/2	*teaspoon New Mexico ground red chile*
1/2	*teaspoon ground cumin*
1/4	*teaspoon salt*
1/4	*teaspoon black pepper, ground fine*
1	*lb. boneless leg of lamb, fat removed, cut into 1/2-inch cubes*
6	*medium red potatoes, cut into 1/2-inch cubes*
1/2	*cup carrots, peeled and diced*
1/2	*cup frozen green peas*
1/4	*cup fresh cilantro, chopped*
2	*cups chicken stock*
4	*cups cooked white rice*

1. In a large Dutch oven or heavy pot, heat oil, add onion, garlic, ground red pepper, cumin, salt and black pepper. Cook until onions are soft.

2. Add lamb and saute for 3 to 4 minutes, or until lightly browned.

3. Add remaining ingredients, bring to a boil, reduce heat, and simmer for 30 to 35 minutes or until potatoes are tender. Serve over warm cooked rice.

Makes 4 servings.

FOUR BEANS & A PEA CASSOULET

Get out your crockpot and let it simmer. When returning from work or play you will have a delightful supper ready.

1	*(16-oz.) can stewed tomatoes undrained, cut up*
1	*(15.5-oz.) can butter beans, drained*
1	*(15.5-oz.) can great northern beans, drained*
1	*(15.5-oz.) can black beans, drained*
1	*(15.5-oz.) can kidney beans, drained*
1	*(15.5-oz.) can garbanzo beans (chick-pea), drained*
1	*cup carrots, finely chopped*
1	*cup white onions, chopped*
2	*garlic cloves, chopped*
2	*NuMex Big Jim green chiles, roasted, peeled, seeded, deveined and finely chopped, or 2 (4-oz.) cans New Mexico green chiles, chopped.*
2	*teaspoons dried-parsley flakes*
1	*teaspoon dried-basil leaves*
1/2	*teaspoon dried-thyme leaves*
1/2	*teaspoon salt*
1/8	*teaspoon fresh ground black pepper*
1	*bay leaf*

1. In a 2-quart slow cooker, combine all ingredients; cover. Cook on high setting for 30 minutes. Reduce to low setting; cook for 5 to 6 hours or until vegetables are tender. Remove bay leaf before serving.

Makes 8 servings.

GRILLED LAMB PATTIES

Sheep ranching is a major livestock activity in New Mexico. Lamb is regularly served with many of our family meals.

1	*lb. ground lamb*
1	*tablespoon canola oil*
6	*tablespoons pinon nuts*
1/4	*teaspoon ground coriander*
1/8	*teaspoon ground cumin*
1	*teaspoon chili powder*
	salt to taste
1/3	*cup ice water*

1. Place meat in a medium-size bowl.

2. In a small skillet, heat oil; saute nuts in oil until they are lightly golden. Drain on paper towels.

3. Mix nuts, coriander, cummin and chili powder with meat. Add salt to taste.

4. Add ice water, a little at a time. Mix until incorporated.

5. Shape into 4 patties; refrigerate 2 hours before grilling.

6. Grill patties, 5 minutes per side.

Makes 4 servings.

GREEN CHILE CHEESEBURGERS

I love to use water soaked hickory chips for grilling. Here is a New Mexico version of an old favorite with a spicy yellow-orange mayonnaise that is colorful and sassy. You may broil if your prefer.

2	*cups hickory chips (if grilling).*
3	*tablespoons low-fat or nonfat plain yogurt*
1	*4(oz.) can New Mexico green chiles, chopped and drained*
1/3	*cup green onions, finely chopped*
1/2	*teaspoon salt*
1/2	*teaspoon black pepper, freshly ground*
2	*lbs lean ground beef*
6	*(oz.) Monterey Jack cheese, cut into 8 slices*
8	*Kaiser rolls split and toasted*
	leaf lettuce
	sliced tomato

SAFFRON MAYONNAISE

1	*egg yolk, room temperature*
2	*cloves garlic, roughly chopped*
1/2	*teaspoon salt, preferably course sea salt*
1/2	*cup olive or peanut oil*
1/2	*teaspoon cayenne pepper*
1/2	*teaspoon saffron threads dissolved in 1 teaspoon hot water*
	lemon juice to taste

1. Soak hickory chips in enough water to cover at least one hour before grilling, if using.

2. In a large mixing bowl, combine yogurt, green chilies, onions, sage and pepper. Add ground beef; mix well. Shape into eight 3/4-inch thick patties.

(Continued on next page)

GREEN CHILE CHEESEBURGERS

(Continued from preceding page)

3. To grill, arrange medium-hot coals around a drip pan in a covered grill. Test for medium heat above pan. Drain hickory chips and place on top of coals. Place burgers on grill rack over the drip pan but not over the coals. Lower the grill hood. Grill burgers until no longer pink, turning once.

4. To broil, place burgers on the unheated rack of a broiler pan. Broil 3 inches from the heat for 15 to 18 minutes or until burgers are no longer pink, turning once.

5. Top each patty with cheese the last 2 minutes of grilling or broiling time. Serve patties on rolls with lettuce, tomato and Saffron Mayonnaise.

Saffron Mayonnaise

1. If the egg is cold from refrigerator, set in bowl of hot water for 1 minute or so to warm it up.

2. Pound the garlic with the salt in a mortar—the coarse grains of the sea salt work especially well for breaking down the garlic—until it forms a smooth paste. Add the egg yolk, and stir briskly for about a minute with the pestle.

3. Whisk in the olive oil or peanut oil as for a mayonnaise, drop by drop as first, then adding it in larger amounts as you go along. When all the oil is incorporated, add the cayenne and the dissolved saffron. Season to taste with lemon juice.

Makes 8 servings.

INDIAN CORN CASSEROLE

Here is a wonderful old way to prepare corn that is as good today as it was 25 years ago when I first prepared it. Even today as soon as my garden corn grows tall I can't wait to get fresh corn and prepare it once again.

4	*ears fresh corn with husks*
3	*cups zucchini, grated*
1	*cup white onion, minced*
1	*(4-oz.) can New Mexican green chiles, chopped*
1/2	*cup all-purpose flour*
1	*teaspoon ground cumin*
1	*teaspoon ground chili powder*
1/4	*teaspoon salt*
1/2	*teaspoon freshly ground black pepper*
1/4	*teaspoon New Mexico red chile powder*
2	*(15.5-oz.) cans black beans, drained*

1. Husk corn, reserving 12 husks; rinse husks thoroughly.

2. In a large saucepan, bring 1 quart of water to a boil; add husks, remove from heat. Cover; and let stand for 15 minutes. Drain; pat dry with paper towels. Line 2-quart baking dish with softened husks, allowing excess to extend over sides.

3. Preheat oven to 325F(165C).

4. Cut whole kernels from 2 ears of corn; set aside. Grate corn from remaining ears, pressing firmly to remove pulp. Add grated corn to cut corn; set aside.

5. In a large non-stick skillet, combine, zucchini, onion, and chiles. Cover and cook over medium-low heat 10 minutes, stirring occasionally. Add flour, cumin, chili powder, salt, ground black pepper and ground red chile; stir well. Add corn and beans; stir. Cook, uncovered, 4 minutes, stirring frequently.

6. Spoon mixture into prepared dish. Fold extended ends of husks toward center, overlapping. Bake for 25 minutes.

Makes 6 servings.

Sassy Southwest Cooking

LIGHT 'N FANCY TOSTADO CUPS

Once in a while, everyone likes to show off and this is one of my best.

1	**lb. beef flank or round steak partially frozen**
6	**(7-inch) flour tortillas**
1	**cup salsa**
1	**teaspoon cornstarch**
1	**medium zucchini, cut into julienne strips about 2 cups**
4	**green onions, sliced**
1	**tablespoon oil**
1/2	**cup Monterey Jack cheese, shredded cherry peppers for garnish (optional) lettuce leaves**

1. Preheat oven to 350F(175C).
2. Slice across grain into bite sized strips. An electric knife may be helpful in slicing the beef. Set aside.
3. For tostada cups, spray a 6-cup muffin tin with non-stick cooking spray. Brush tortillas lightly with warm water or soften in microwave. Starting at the outer edge of each tortilla and going toward center, cut four-inch long slits in spoke-like fashion. Gently press tortilla into muffin tin, overlapping edges to form cups. Bake for 12 to 15 minutes or until crisp. Remove from cups and set aside.
4. Combine salsa and cornstarch and set aside.
5. Spray a large skillet with vegetable spray; preheat. Add zucchini cook and stir over high heat 1-1/2 minutes. Add onions cook until soft. Remove vegetables from skillet.
6. Add oil to skillet and cook beef 1/2 at a time 2 to 3 minutes or until done. Return all beef to skillet. Stir in salsa, cook and stir until thickened and bubbly. Cook an additional 2 minutes longer.
7. Stir in vegetables. Place each tostada cup on lettuce lined serving plates. Spoon in meat mixture and top with cheese. Garnish with cherry peppers (optional).

Makes 6 servings.

MILLIE'S BRISKET

No one fixes better brisket than my wife, Millie. The secret is a tight seal, retaining the moisture.

2	*beef bullion cubes*
2	*cups hot water*
1/4	*cup light-sodium reduced soy sauce*
3	*tablespoons Liquid Smoke*
1	*(4-5 lb.) beef brisket*
	garlic powder to taste

1. In saucepan dissolve bullion cubes in hot water, add soy sauce and Liquid Smoke. Set aside.

2. Place brisket in dutch oven. Sprinkle with garlic powder. Pour bullion mixture over brisket and cover with foil, place lid over foil, making a tight seal.

3. In a preheated 300F (150C) oven, bake for 6 hours. Refrigerate until 1 hour before serving time. Slice cross grain and re-heat to serve.

Makes 8 servings.

NOTE: This brisket is best if prepared a day ahead.

 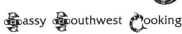

MUSHROOM & PEPPER QUESADILLAS

Quesadillas can be made with many combinations of ingredients. Have fun creating your own combinations.

2 *tablespoons oil*
1 *white onion, finely chopped*
1 *lb. fresh mushrooms, sliced*
1 *garlic clove, minced*
1 *tablespoon fresh oregano, minced*
1 *(10.5-oz.) can tomato soup*
8 *(10-inch) flour tortillas*
2 *red bell peppers, seeded and finely sliced*
2 *New Mexican chiles, roasted, peeled, seeded, deveined and finely chopped*
2 *cups Monterey Jack cheese, grated*
   Sour cream
   Fresh Basil Salsa (page 143)

1. Preheat oven to 350F(175C).

2. In large skillet heat oil; add onion, mushrooms and oregano. Stir frequently, cook until onion is soft.

3. Stir in tomato soup and heat thoroughly.

4. Place 4 tortillas on a lightly greased baking sheet and spoon tomato mixture onto them. Top with bell peppers, chiles and cheese, top with another tortilla.

5. Bake for 10 minutes or until cheese is melted.

6. Cut into quarters and serve immediately, with sour cream and salsa.

Makes 4 servings.

NEW MEXICAN MEAT FILLING

This meat filling freezes well and will save you time in the preparation of the numerous recipes. It's a must in New Mexico kitchens.

5	*lbs. beef roast*
3	*tablespoons oil*
2	*white onions, chopped*
1	*(4-oz.) can New Mexico green chiles, chopped*
2	*(7-oz.) cans green chile salsa*
1/4	*teaspoon garlic powder*
4	*tablespoons all-purpose flour*
4	*teaspoons salt*
1	*teaspoon ground cumin*
	juices from roast

1. Preheat oven to 350F(175C). Place roast in 4-6-quart baking dish, cover and roast 2-1/2 hours or until well done. Drain the meat, reserving juices. Cool and remove fat and bones. Shred meat and set aside.

2. In a large skillet, heat oil, add onions and green chiles. Saute for 1 minute. Stir in salsa, garlic powder, flour, salt, and cumin. Cook for 1 minute longer. Stir in reserved meat juices and shredded meat. Cook 5 minutes or until thickened. Use at once or pack into freezer containers.

Makes about 9 cups.

Simplify meal preparation. Here is a spicy meat filling that can be used in a number of dishes. Used as a filling for burritos, tamales, tostados and flautas, it will save you valuable time.

POSOLE

My first taste of this dish was in Taos and this is the same recipe. I have prepared it many times and although I have since found many more versions, this one is still special to me.

1	*pork loin roast, about 3 lbs*
5	*cups water*
3	*cups chicken broth*
2	*cups onion, chopped*
2	*teaspoons salt*
1	*whole chicken, about 2-1/2 lbs.*
2	*garlic, cloves, crushed*
1-1/2	*tablespoons chili powder*
1/2	*teaspoon paprika*
1-1/2	*tablespoons bacon grease*
2	*(16 oz.) cans white hominy, drained*

Garnishes:
   chopped white onions
   sliced radishes
   sliced avocado
   lime wedges

1. In a large Dutch oven, place pork roast and water. Bring to a boil. Add onions and salt. Reduce heat, cover and simmer gently for 30 minutes. Add chicken and bring to a boil, reduce heat, cover and simmer for 45 minutes. Remove pork and chicken from broth and allow to cool. Cover and refrigerate broth.
2. Cut pork and chicken meat into small pieces and discard bones.
3. In skillet heat bacon grease, add garlic, chili powder, and paprika; stir just until blended. Add small amount of broth and stir. Add mixture and hominy to broth and bring to a boil. Reduce heat, cover and simmer gently for 30 minutes; add pork and chicken pieces and simmer until meat is thoroughly heated, about 15 minutes. Serve in individual bowls with garnishes as side dishes.

Makes 8 servings.

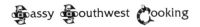

STUFFED MEXICAN CABBAGE

Another contribution from the Germanic community in Albuquerque. A good example of the cultural blending which produces some of New Mexico's unusual fare.

1	*medium head cabbage*
1/2	*lb. pork sausage*
1	*lb. ground beef*
1	*onion, grated*
1-1/2	*cups chopped, roasted, peeled, seeded green chiles*
1/2	*teaspoon garlic salt*
1-1/2	*cups thinly sliced, peeled apples*
1	*onion, chopped*
1	*(16-oz.) can sauerkraut, rinsed, drained*
1	*cup chicken broth*
1	*cup tomato juice*

1. Core cabbage. Place in a large pot and cover with boiling water; simmer for 5 minutes. Remove cabbage from water and cool. Pull leaves off one at a time; you should have about 10 large leaves. Trim away vein end of leaves.

2. In a skillet, combine sausage and ground beef and cook 15 to 20 minutes. Add grated onion and cook until onion is clear. Drain off excess fat. Add green chiles and garlic salt; mix well. Cool.

3. Place 1/3 cup of meat and chile mixture near the vein of the leaf. Fold the end over the stuffing; fold over the sides, envelope-fashion, and roll as tightly as possible.

4. Preheat oven to 350F(175C). In a bowl, mix apples, chopped onion and sauerkraut. Spread half of this mixture on the bottom of deep baking dish or casserole. Place cabbage rolls on sauerkraut. Spread remaining mixture on top.

5. Mix broth and tomato juice, pour over rolls. Cover and bake in preheated oven 1 hour.

Makes 4 to 5 servings.

SPANISH CHICKEN SKILLET SUPPER

This is one that features pecans. I am constantly amazed at the many uses for this popular nut. I hope you give this one a try. I recommend it highly.

> 2 *tablespoons butter*
> 1/2 *cup coarsely chopped pecans*
> 1 *cup instant rice long grain*
> 1 *garlic clove, minced*
> 1 *(14.5-oz.) can stewed tomatoes*
> 1 *(14-oz.) can chicken broth*
> 1 *teaspoon chili powder*
> 1/2 *teaspoon ground cumin*
> 1/2 *teaspoon salt*
> 1 *cup cooked chicken, diced*
> 1/2 *small zucchini halved lengthwise, cut into 1/2-inch slices*
> 1/2 *cup green onions, sliced with tops*
> 1 *(4-oz.) can New Mexico green chile, chopped*
> 1/2 *cup Monterey Jack cheese, shredded*
> 2 *tablespoons fresh cilantro, chopped*

1. In large skillet heat butter. Add pecans, cook until lightly toasted. Remove and drain on paper towels and set aside.

2. Add rice and garlic to skillet; cook and stir for 1 minute. Add tomatoes, chicken broth, chili powder, cumin and salt. Bring to a boil; reduce heat. Cover tightly and simmer 15 minutes.

3. Add chicken pieces, zucchini, onions, and green chile; cover and continue to simmer 5 minutes. Remove from heat; let stand covered for 5 minutes or until liquid is absorbed. Sprinkle with shredded cheese, reserved pecans and cilantro.

Makes 4 servings.

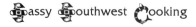

VAQUERO BREAKFAST

Hard work requires a hearty breakfast. This one fills the bill if you are looking for a solid New Mexico way to start the day.

4	*8-inch flour tortillas*
2	*cups chili of your choice*
1	*teaspoon butter*
3	*medium Russet potatoes*
4	*large eggs*
1	*cup ripe tomatoes, chopped*
1/2	*cup sliced green onions, with a few tops*
1/2	*cup Cheddar cheese, shredded*
1	*cup salsa of choice*
	salt to taste

1. Preheat oven to 400F(200C).

2. Cook, peel and dice potatoes.

3. Rub both sides of tortillas with butter and place into 2 loaf pans (2 tortillas per pan). Gently shape each to create a bowl.

4. In a medium sauce pan, heat chili. Stir in pre-cooked potatoes and cook until thoroughly heated.

5. Divide chili and place on shaped tortillas. With back of tablespoons, make an indentation in each chili mixture.

6. Break egg into each indentation. Bake 10 minutes. Cover loosely with foil. Bake 5 to 10 minutes longer or until eggs are done.

7. Gently lift each bowl from loaf pan and place on serving plate. Spoon on tomatoes and onions. Sprinkle with cheese. Serve with salsa.

Makes 4 servings.

VEGETABLES & SIDE DISHES

Like many other ethnic-based cuisines, New Mexico's food is going through a period of change. The rich cultural transition that New Mexico is currently experiencing is starting to have an effect on our food. For centuries New Mexico cuisine has been based on Native American and Spanish influences. With an ever-increasing percentage of Anglo and Asian population, new foods are appearing regularly. Nowhere is it more noticeable than in new vegetables and side dishes. The arrival of many imported vegetables, new fruits and reduced fat awareness has contributed to many new dishes. However, I still prefer the old faithfuls like corn, squash and pinto beans.

I present a number of unusual combinations of traditional staples which feature corn, beans and squash. I think you will like them. These versions of old traditional dishes will add spice, color and texture to your meals.

ANASAZI BEANS WITH CHILES & TOMATOES

Try these speckled beauties, they cook faster and are sweeter than pinto beans.

2	**cups dry Anasazi beans**
6	**cups water**
2	**tablespoons vegetable oil**
1/2	**small white onion, chopped**
1	**garlic clove, chopped**
1	**(14.5-oz.) can tomatoes, chopped**
1/4	**teaspoon ground cumin**
1	**(4-oz.) can New Mexico chiles, chopped**
1/2	**cup vegetable broth**
	salt and pepper to taste

1. Rinse beans, place in Dutch oven or heavy pot, cover with water. Cook about 2 hours until beans are soft, adding water as necessary. Drain and cool.

2. Heat oil in heavy skillet. Add onions and garlic and cook until soft. Add tomatoes with liquid, vegetable broth, and cumin bring to a boil and reduce heat. Cover and simmer 5 minutes stirring occasionally.

3. Add beans and chiles to mixture and cook on low 10 minutes. Season with salt and pepper to taste.

Makes 4 to 6 servings.

The Anasazi culture existed from before the first century A.D. to the fourteenth century. They abandoned their massive pueblos in about the late 1200's. They mastered stonemasonry, surface mining, water control systems, road engineering and pottery.

BAKED BEANS NEW MEXICO STYLE

These are certainly not Boston Baked Beans but have a special flavor all their own. As a rule I always cook dry beans in distilled water, try it and see if you notice the difference.

1	*lb. dried pinto beans*
6	*cups distilled water*
2	*tablespoons chicken-flavored bouillon granules*
1	*(12-oz.) bottle dark beer*
1	*medium onion, chopped*
6	*cloves garlic, minced*
3	*jalapeño peppers, seeded and minced*
1/4	*cup Three Chile Sauce (page 137)*
3	*tablespoons brown sugar, packed firm*
3	*tablespoons vinegar*
1-1/2	*tablespoons Worcestershire sauce*
1/2	*teaspoon ground cinnamon*
1/4	*cup Red Chile Sauce (page 134)*

1. Rinse beans, remove debris or broken beans, cover with at least 1 inch of water. Remove any floating beans and let them sit overnight. Drain and rinse well. Set aside.

2. In an 8-quart Dutch oven, combine 6 cups distilled water, bouillon granules, dark beer, onions, garlic, and add reserved beans. Bring to a boil. Lower heat, cover and cook beans gently for 2 hours, stirring occasionally.

3. Stir in jalapeño peppers; simmer, uncovered, 30 minutes or until beans are tender. In a preheated 350F(175C), bake uncovered for 30 minutes.

4. Top with Red Chile Sauce (page 134) and serve.

Makes 6-8 servings.

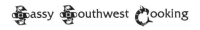 assy outhwest ooking

BAKED NUMEX BIG JIM CHILE RELLENOS W/CORN STUFFING

I love chile rellenos but the fried version has too high a fat content for me. Here's the way I enjoy them now. If you are trying to cut back on fat, try these.

2	*tablespoons butter*
1	*medium white onion, chopped*
1	*garlic clove, minced*
3	*cups fresh or frozen whole-kernel corn, thawed*
1	*large ripe red tomato, peeled and chopped*
1/4	*teaspoon salt*
1/8	*teaspoon fresh ground black pepper*
1/8	*teaspoon ground oregano*
3	*cups Monterey jack cheese, shredded*
12	*NuMex Big Jim New Mexico chiles, roasted, peeled, seeded, deveined (if not available try fresh poblano or Anaheim chiles) Red Chile Sauce (page 134)*

1. After roasting and peeling, prepare chiles by making a small slit on each chile to remove the seeds and veins.

2. Preheat oven to 350F(175C) and grease a large shallow baking dish.

3. In large skillet heat butter. Add onions and garlic and cook until onions until soft. Add corn, tomato, salt, pepper and oregano and simmer, uncovered, 15 to 20 minutes. Remove from heat. Stir in 2 cups of shredded cheese; cool.

4. Stuff chiles with corn mixture and place in a prepared baking dish and sprinkle with remaining cheese. Bake uncovered 25 minutes or until sauce is bubbly and cheese is lightly browned. Spoon Red Chile Sauce down the center of the chiles and serve.

Makes 4 to 6 servings.

CHILE SOUFFLE

This souffle can be easily prepared for two by splitting into four small casserole dishes. Freeze two unbaked then later, just thaw them and bake as directed.

3	*tablespoons butter*
3	*tablespoons all purpose flour*
1	*cup whole milk*
3	*egg yolks*
1/2	*cup cottage cheese*
1/2	*cup tomatoes chopped, drained*
2	*tablespoons green onions, chopped*
1	*(4-oz) can New Mexico green chiles, chopped*
	salt
	fresh ground black pepper
4	*egg whites*

1. Preheat oven 350F(175C).

2. In a saucepan melt butter and stir in flour. Using a whisk, blend in milk. Over medium heat, cover and cook until thick. Remove from heat and whisk in egg yolks one at a time. Fold in cottage cheese, tomatoes, onions, chiles. Salt and pepper to taste.

3. In medium bowl, beat egg whites until they form stiff peaks. Thoroughly fold about 1/2 of egg whites into yolk mixture. Add remaining whites and fold in quickly, leaving some streaks of the whites showing.

4. Pour mixture into one-quart souffle dish. To make the center rise higher than the edges, run a finger around inner rim of the dish to make a trough for the egg mixture. Bake 30-35 minutes, until deep golden brown.

Makes 4 servings

FIESTA CORN

Quick and easy, this is a side dish you will serve again and again.

2	*cups fresh or frozen corn kernels*
1/4	*cup water*
1/4	*cup New Mexico green chiles, roasted, peeled, deveined, seeded and chopped*
2	*tablespoons green olives, chopped*
2	*green onions, diced*

1. Cook corn in water for 6 to 8 minutes over medium heat.

2. Drain and add chiles, green olives and onions.

3. Stir and cook briefly until thoroughly warmed.

Makes 4 servings.

"Red or Green?" This question is the most commonly asked question in New Mexican restaurants. It is not an easy answer because different cooks prepare sauces to satisfy their own taste. Generally red chile is milder. The green chile is the immature chile and the red is the mature. Red chile tends to have a richer, fuller flavor. The green has a sharper, clearer bite.

Sassy Southwest Cooking

FRIED GREEN TOMATOES WITH CHILE

Corn meal and chiles give an unexpected taste to this adaptation of an old Southern dish that is sure to please.

3/4	*cup finely ground cornmeal*
1/2	*teaspoon salt*
1-1/4	*lbs. green tomatoes*
2	*tablespoons butter*
4	*New Mexico green chile, roasted, peeled, seeded, deveined and chopped.*

1. In a shallow bowl, combine cornmeal and salt.

2. Cut tomatoes into 1/2-inch strips. Dip each slice in cornmeal, make sure it is completely covered.

3. In heavy skillet melt butter. Over medium heat cook tomato slices until brown on both sides. Spread chiles evenly over the tomato slices, cover and steam 5 minutes or chiles are hot.

Makes 4 to 6 servings.

The tomato, native to south America, became popular in the U.S in the 1900s. The green tomato has a piquant flavor which makes it excellent for frying, broiling or adding to salsas. Dozens of varieties are available today—ranging widely in size and shape. The most common tomato used in New Mexican cooking is the beefsteak tomato which is delicious both raw and cooked.

FRIED SQUASH FLOWERS

The blossoms of either summer or winter squash are edible and delicious. They are very perishable and should be refrigerated for no longer than a day.

1   *cup Parmesan cheese, grated*
1   *cup ricotta cheese, crumbled*
2   *red bell peppers, roasted, peeled, seeded and diced*
2   *oz. sun-dried tomatoes, reconstituted and diced*
2   *tablespoons fresh basil, chopped*
12   *large squash flowers, tightly closed*
2   *eggs*
2   *tablespoons water*
1/2   *cup all-purpose flour*
      salt and fresh ground black pepper to taste
1/2   *cup peanut oil*

1. In a medium bowl combine 1/2 cup Parmesan cheese, ricotta cheese, bell peppers, reconstituted tomatoes and basil. Mix thoroughly.

2. Gently open flowers and stuff each with cheese mixture, closing flower around the stuffing.

3. In a small bowl whisk the eggs with water.

4. In another small bowl combine remaining Parmesan cheese, salt and pepper to taste.

5. Dip flowers in egg mixture, then coat with cheese mixture.

6. In a large skillet or Dutch oven heat oil. Saute, flowers about 1 minute, or until golden brown. Drain on paper towels.

Makes 4 servings.

GREEN BEANS IN JALAPEÑO DRESSING

I like green beans fixed this attractive way. The zest of the lime and the fire of the jalapeño pepper add new life to fresh green beans.

1-1/2	*lb. fresh green beans*
1	*cup water*
1	*egg yolk*
1/4	*cup lime juice*
1	*jalapeño chile, seeded and chopped*
2	*tablespoons olive oil*
1	*tablespoon sugar*
1	*tablespoon prepared mustard*
2	*teaspoons grated lime rind*
1/4	*teaspoon fresh ground black pepper*
2	*medium oranges, cut into wedges*

1. Rinse and trim beans; cut into lengths to fit the width of food processor food chute. Position slicer disk in food processor; stack beans on their sides in the food chute. Using gentle pressure, push and slice beans. Repeat with remaining beans.

2. Place beans and water in 3-quart saucepan. Bring to boil. Cover and reduce heat; simmer 2 minutes or until beans are tender. Drain beans and arrange on serving platter.

3. Place egg yolk, lime juice, jalapeño pepper, olive oil, sugar, mustard, lime peel, and pepper in food processor bowl. Process until blended.

4. Arrange orange wedges around the beans, and top with dressing. Serve immediately.

Makes 6 servings.

GRILLED SPANISH STYLE EGGPLANT

Try to choose the youngest eggplant you can find. As the plant matures, the skin becomes tough and the eggplant tends to be bitter.

2	*small eggplants*
2	*tablespoons garlic cloves, chopped*
2	*jalapeño chiles, seeded and finely minced*
1	*teaspoon red chile powder*
1/2	*cup light soy sauce*
1/4	*cup toasted sesame oil*

1. Slice eggplants lengthwise into 1/8-inch thick pieces. Sprinkle with salt and set aside for 20 minutes. Pat with paper towel to remove excess moisture. This helps eliminate some of the acid taste.

2. In a large bowl combine garlic, jalapeños, chile peppers, chili powder, soy sauce and toasted sesame oil. Whisk together. Add eggplant slices and marinate 4 to 6 hours.

3. Heat a large non-stick skillet, cook slices for 3 or 4 minutes on each side until lightly browned.

Makes 4 servings.

The eggplant is a member of the nightshade family and is related to the tomato and potato. Though commonly thought of as a vegetable, it is actually a fruit. It's a good source of folic acid and potassium. Its sponge-like structure causes it to absorb fat or oil.

INDIAN CORN PUDDING

I first tasted this pudding many years ago in Albuquerque. It is one you acquire a taste for and once hooked, you will want it again and again.

3	**tablespoons butter or margarine**
1	**small white onion, chopped**
1/2	**garlic clove, minced**
1	**medium green bell pepper, seeded and chopped**
1/4	**cup all-purpose flour**
1/2	**teaspoon salt**
1	**teaspoon sugar**
1/8	**teaspoon fresh ground black pepper**
1	**(16-oz.) can cream-style corn**
3	**eggs, lightly beaten**
1	**cup milk**

1. Preheat oven to 350F(175C). Butter a 2-quart dish and set aside.

2. In saucepan, heat butter or margarine; add onion, garlic and bell pepper. Cook, stirring often, 5 minutes until onion is soft. Stir in flour, salt, sugar, and pepper; cook, stirring, until thickened.

3. Remove from heat, add corn, eggs and milk. Stirring until mixture is well-blended.

4. Pour mixture into prepared baking dish. Bake uncovered about 55 minutes until center is set. Test by gently shaking dish.

Makes 4 servings.

REFRIED BEANS

Refried beans are an important ingredient in many New Mexican meals. Here is a way to enjoy them with lowered fat content.

4	**oz. coarsely chopped bacon**
2	**chopped, white onions**
2	**garlic cloves, minced**
4	**cups cooked pinto or black beans or 2 (15.5-oz.) cans of beans.**
1/2	**cup low-sodium chicken broth**
2	**tablespoons white vinegar**
	Fresh ground black pepper to taste

1. Heat a large non-stick skillet, fry bacon about 4 minutes, stirring frequently until it begins to brown. Drain and return 1 tablespoon of drippings to skillet.

2. Add onions and garlic and cook 6 or 7 minutes until onions are soft and bacon is browned.

3. If using canned beans, drain and reserve 1/2 cup of liquid.

4. To skillet, add beans and broth or reserved liquid. Coarsely mash beans; season to taste with vinegar and black pepper.

Makes 6 servings.

Although the pinto bean is king in New Mexico, many other beans are a part of today's delicious taste treats. Many more varieties are used than in the past, among the most popular are Lima, black, Anasazi, red kidney, and garbanzo or chick-pea.

SASSY STUFFED TOMATOES

Colorful and excellent eating, this is the kind of dish that will give you a reputation for being a great cook.

4	*medium firm tomatoes*
1/2	*cup dairy sour cream*
3	*tablespoons jalapeño chile, seeded and chopped*
3	*tablespoons green bell peppers, seeded and chopped*
3	*tablespoons green onions, sliced*
2	*tablespoons all-purpose flour*
3/4	*teaspoon sugar*
1/2	*teaspoon salt*
1	*oz. Monterey Jack cheese, shredded*
1/4	*cup Cheddar cheese, shredded*
	Jalapeño chile slices for garnish

1. Cut 1/4-inch slice from the stem end of each tomato. If necessary, cut a thin slice off the other end so that tomatoes will sit upright. Using a teaspoon, gently remove the seeds and juice of each tomato. Place tomatoes upside down on paper towels to drain.

2. In a small bowl, combine sour cream, peppers, onions, flour, sugar, and salt; mix well.

3. Place tomatoes upright on a foil-lined broiler pan or baking sheet. Spoon sour cream mixture into tomatoes. Broil 3 to 5 inches from heat for 2 to 3 minutes or until sour cream is bubbly and lightly browned. Sprinkle tomatoes with cheeses; broil 2 to 3 minutes longer until cheese is melted. Garnish with jalapeño chiles if desired.

Makes 4 servings.

SPANISH RICE

The perfect accompaniment for beef, chicken or seafood.

4	*tablespoons vegetable oil*
2	*tablespoons butter*
2	*cups long grain rice*
1	*large white onion, chopped*
2	*garlic cloves, minced*
2	*New Mexico chiles, roasted, peeled, seeded, deveined, chopped, or 1 (4-oz.) can diced green chiles*
3/4	*pound tomatoes, peeled, seeded, and chopped*
4	*cups chicken broth*
1/8	*teaspoon dry-leaf oregano*
1/4	*cup tomato puree*
	fresh ground black pepper to taste
1/4	*cup fresh cilantro, chopped*

1. In a large sauce pan, heat butter and oil. When butter is melted, add rice. Stirring constantly, cook 3 to 4 minutes until lightly browned.

2. Add onion, garlic, chiles, and oregano; cook for additional 5 minutes, stirring frequently.

3. Add tomatoes, tomato puree, and chicken broth. Bring to a boil; reduce heat, cover, and simmer about 20 minutes until liquid is absorbed and rice is tender. Remove from heat and stir in cilantro.

Makes 6 servings.

SPICY GARBANZO BEANS & VEGETABLES

From Roman times, the garbanzo or chick-pea has been an important food. Here it is all dressed up in a New Mexico dish served over rice.

1	tablespoon olive oil
1/2	cup sliced white onion
2	garlic cloves, finely chopped
2	cups sliced carrots
4	cups sliced zucchini
1	(15.5-oz.) can garbanzo beans, undrained
1	(4-oz.) can New Mexico green chiles, chopped
1	teaspoon chicken bullion granules
1/2	teaspoon salt
2	cups hot cooked rice
1	teaspoon fresh cilantro, minced

1. Heat oil in a 3-quart saucepan. Add onion and garlic and cook until soft.

2. Stir in remaining ingredients except rice and cilantro. Bring to boil, stirring occasionally; reduce heat. Cover and simmer for 12 to 14 minutes or until vegetables are crisp-tender. Serve over hot rice. Garnish with cilantro.

Makes 4 servings.

SQUASH & TOMATO CON QUESO

Con queso means with cheese. The tart flavor of chevre (goat) cheese is the secret of this dish. It delivers an unexpected flavor.

4	*cups water*
4	*medium yellow crook neck squash*
2	*large ripe tomatoes*
1/4	*cup fresh dillweed, minced*
2	*tablespoons fresh basil leaves, minced*
2	*Hungarian yellow wax peppers seeded and sliced into rings*
1	*cup (8-oz.) chevre (goat) cheese, crumbled*

1. Preheat oven to 400F (200C).

2. Heat water in a 2-quart saucepan. Add squash, bring to a boil. Reduce heat; simmer 2 to 3 minutes until tender.

3. Remove from heat; drain immediately. Rinse with cold water. Cut into 1/4-inch slices. Set aside.

4. Trim both ends from tomatoes, and discard. Cut tomato in half crosswise to form 2 thick slices each; set aside.

5. Cut four 12-inch pieces of heavy-duty foil. Place 1 tomato slice on each piece. Place squash slices on tomatoes. Sprinkle with dillweed and basil. Top with pepper rings and chevre cheese.

6. Fold to seal packets, place on baking sheet. Bake for 15 to 20 minutes. Serve immediately.

Makes 4 servings.

Chevre cheese is pure white goat cheese. It has a delightfully tart flavor that easily distinguishes it from other cheeses. It can range in texture from moist and creamy to dry and semi-firm. It comes in a variety of shapes and takes on a sour taste when it is old. After opening always wrap it tightly and store in refrigerator.

CHILI

Any New Mexico cookbook can be considered incomplete without chili recipes. In the U.S. some people consider chili cooking as a national pastime. Thousands of dollars in prize money provide incentive for real competition. Chile-mania is becoming an obsession to more chili-lovers each year. I no longer compete but still enjoy visiting and judging chili cookoffs. These cooks are a warm, fun-loving group and I especially appreciate the recipes I have received from "Chiliheads" since the publication of my first cookbook.

In this chapter, you will find easy and unusual chili dishes starting with the original "Bowl of Red." Included are chicken and turkey dishes and some new variations on old themes. There is even a Competition Chili. This recipe has won in several chili cookoffs.

With all the attention chili is getting, I hope that the Bowl of Red will not get lost in the shuffle. It is, and always will be, real chili to me.

BOWL OF RED

Here is my favorite. The dish that may have started the chili-mania.

2	*tablespoons vegetable oil*
1	*large white onion, coarsely chopped*
3	*garlic cloves, finely chopped*
3	*lbs. lean beef, coarse grind*
4	*tablespoons ground hot New Mexico red chile*
4	*tablespoons ground mild New Mexico red chile*
2	*teaspoons ground cumin*
1-1/2	*teaspoons salt*
3	*cups water*

1. In a 4-quart Dutch oven or heavy pot, heat oil; add onion and garlic. Cook until soft.

2. Add beef, ground chiles, and cumin; cook until meat is evenly browned, breaking any lumps with fork.

3. Add salt and water, bring to a boil; and reduce heat. Simmer uncovered 2 to 3 hours; stirring occasionally, until meat is very tender and flavors are fully blended. Add more water as necessary.

Makes 6 servings.

The exact origin of chili is still debated today, but New Mexicans claim it was a chuckwagon cook who ran out of black pepper. Looking for a substitute, he tried the little red peppers commonly used by the local Indians and Mexicans and thus "Bowl of Red" was born. Purists say "if you want chili, make chili, if you want beans, cook beans." In New Mexico we have no such prejudices, some even say that chili tastes better with beans.

BRISKET CHILI

A delicious, chili made from brisket, needs to be cooked slowly. I add beans for extra fullness and flavor.

	vegetable cooking spray
2	*lbs. lean brisket, cut into 1/2-inch cubes*
2	*cups white onion, chopped*
1	*cup green bell pepper, seeded and chopped*
3	*fresh Serrano chile peppers, seeded and finely chopped*
3	*cloves garlic, minced*
2	*tablespoons chili powder*
1	*teaspoon ground cumin*
1/2	*teaspoon dried-leaf oregano*
1/4	*teaspoon ground New Mexico red pepper*
1/3	*cup masa harina or cornmeal*
1	*(14.5-oz.) can whole tomatoes, chopped*
1	*(13.5-oz.) can beef broth*
1	*(12-oz.) can beer*
2	*tablespoons white vinegar*
	salt to taste

1. Coat a large Dutch oven with cooking spray; heat until hot. Add brisket and cook 5 minutes stirring frequently, until browned. Drain well. Set aside. Wipe drippings from Dutch oven with a paper towel.

2. Recoat Dutch oven with cooking spray. Add onion, bell pepper, Serrano pepper and garlic; saute 5 minutes or until soft.

3. Return brisket to Dutch oven, add chili powder, cumin, oregano, and red chile pepper; stir well. Sprinkle mixture with masa harina; stir well. Add tomatoes, beef broth and beer; bring to a boil.

4. Reduce heat, and simmer partially covered, 1-1/2 hours. Add vinegar, and simmer partially covered, 30 minutes or until meat is tender.

Makes 8 servings.

CHICKEN & RICE CHILI

One of the most unusual chili recipes, surprisingly good, very good! It is also very low fat and low calorie.

1	*tablespoon oil of choice*
1-1/2	*pounds chicken thighs, skinned, boned, meat cut into 1/2-inch pieces*
1	*medium white onion, chopped*
1/2	*cup long grain rice, uncooked*
2	*(16-oz.) cans stewed tomatoes*
1	*(14.5-oz.) can low-salt chicken broth*
1-1/4	*cups water*
1	*(15.5-oz.) can pinto beans, drained and rinsed*
1	*tablespoon chili powder*
1/8	*teaspoon salt*
1/8	*teaspoon ground black pepper*

1. In 4-quart Dutch oven or heavy pot, heat oil. Over medium-high heat, cook chicken 5 to 8 minutes or until browned, stirring frequently.

2. Add onion; cook 3 to 5 minutes or until onion is soft. Add remaining ingredients. Bring to a boil and reduce heat to medium; cover and cook 25 to 40 minutes or until rice is tender and chicken is no longer pink.

Makes 5 to 6 servings.

Sassy Southwest Cooking

CHILI VERDE

This traditional recipe is one of my oldest and best.

1	*pound lean boneless pork shoulder*
1	*(28-oz.) can tomatoes*
2	*medium white onions, chopped*
1-1/2	*cups celery thinly sliced*
1	*teaspoon dried-leaf oregano*
1/2	*teaspoon powdered sage*
2	*bay leaves*
1	*large green bell pepper, seeded and chopped*
3	*New Mexico green chile peppers, roasted, peeled, seeded and chopped*
4	*cups cooked white rice*
	salt
	fresh ground black pepper
	Cilantro

1. Trim all fat from pork and cut into 3/4-inch cubes.

2. In a large Dutch oven or heavy pot, add pork and 1/3 of the liquid from tomatoes. Bring to rolling boil; reduce heat and simmer covered for 30 minutes.

3. Uncover pot; add onions, celery, oregano, and sage. Cook over high heat, stirring frequently until liquid has evaporated and pan drippings are browned (8 to 10 minutes). Add bay leaves.

4. Stir in tomatoes and remaining liquid, break tomatoes up with a spoon. Make sure to scrape any browned bits free from pan. Reduce heat, cover and simmer for 30 minutes. Stir in bell peppers and chiles; cover again and continue to simmer, stirring occasionally, until meat is very tender. Continue to simmer uncovered until mixture is as thick as you like.

5. Remove bay leaves. Spoon over rice and garnish with sprigs of Cilantro.

Makes 4 servings.

CHORIZO CHILI

Chorizo may be new for you, be adventurous and try this highly seasoned Mexican sausage the next time you make chili.

1/2	*lb. chorizo sausage, slightly frozen*
2	*tablespoons oil*
2	*small white onions, chopped*
2	*small green bell peppers, seeded and chopped*
3	*garlic cloves, minced*
3	*(15-oz.) cans whole tomatoes, cut up*
3	*(8-oz.) cans tomato sauce*
2	*(10.5-oz.) cans condensed beef broth*
1	*(12-oz.) can beer*
2	*(4-oz.) cans green chiles chopped, undrained*
2	*tablespoons chili powder*
1/2	*tablespoon ground cumin*
1	*teaspoon cayenne pepper*
1/2	*teaspoon dried-leaf oregano*
1/2	*teaspoon cinnamon*
3	*(15.5-oz.) cans of kidney beans, drained and rinsed*
6	*tablespoons Cheddar cheese, shredded*

1. In a large Dutch oven or heavy pot, heat oil. Add onions, sausage and cook until onions are soft, drain.

2. Add remaining ingredients except beans and cheese; bring to boil; reduce heat. Simmer uncovered for 1-1/2 to 2 hours, stirring occasionally.

3. Add kidney beans; simmer until thoroughly heated. Garnish as desired with cheese.

Makes 10 to 12 servings.

COMPETITION CHILI

If you would like to enter a chili cookoff, this is a proven winner. With little modification, you might win.

3	lbs. sirloin tip, course ground or cut into small pieces
2	teaspoons vegetable oil
1	white onion, chopped
1	(14.5-oz.) can beef broth
1/2	teaspoon dried-leaf oregano
3-1/2	tablespoons ground cumin, divided
6	cloves garlic, chopped, divided
1	teaspoon mild New Mexico ground chile powder, divided
5	teaspoons hot New Mexico ground chile powder, divided
1	(8-oz.) can tomato sauce
1	(14.5-oz.) can chicken broth
1	teaspoon Tabasco pepper sauce
1	teaspoon brown sugar
1	tablespoon lime juice
	dash of MSG
	salt to taste

1. In a large Dutch oven or heavy pot heat oil. Cook meat until lightly browned.

2. Add onion and beef broth to cover meat. Bring to a boil and cook for 15 minutes. Add oregano and cumin, garlic, and 1/2 chile powders. Reduce heat to medium and cook for 10 minutes.

3. Add tomato sauce, remaining garlic, remaining beef broth and the chicken broth for desired consistency. Cook for one hour over medium heat, stirring occasionally.

4. Add remaining chile powders and cumin. Simmer 25 minutes, stirring occasionally.

5. Add Tabasco sauce, brown sugar, lime juice and salt to taste. Simmer to desired consistency.

Makes 8 servings.

EASY CHIPOTLE CHILI

The sweet smoky flavor of the Chipotle chile imparts an unusual taste. I have learned to like the Chipotle and also use it in mole sauces.

4	*dried-Chipotle chiles*
2	*teaspoons vegetable oil*
1/2	*medium white onion, coarsely chopped*
2	*garlic cloves, minced*
1	*lb. lean beef, coarse grind*
1/4	*teaspoon dried-leaf oregano*
1/4	*teaspoon ground cumin*
2	*(10-oz.) cans tomato soup*
1	*(10.5-oz.) can onion soup*
2	*(16-oz.) cans kidney beans, drained*

1. Cover chiles with warm water. Let stand for 1 hour until softened. Drain and finely chop.

2. In a 4-quart Dutch oven or heavy pot, heat oil; add onion and garlic. Cook until soft.

3. Add meat, chiles, oregano, cumin. Cook, breaking up meat, stirring frequently until meat is brown.

4. Stir in tomato and onion soups, and beans. Bring to a boil and reduce heat. Simmer 1/2 hour or to desired consistency.

Makes 4 servings.

Many chile varieties are grown in New Mexico, such as New Mexican, jalapeño, cayenne, ancho, pasilla, mirasol, and del arbol. New Mexican-type cultivars include 'NuMex R Naky', 'NuMex Big Jim', 'Sandia', 'NuMex Conquistador', 'NuMex Sweet', 'NuMex 6-4', and 'NuMex Joe Parker'. Each has its own heat level and taste.

JALAPEÑO CHILI

America's favorite chile pepper adds real heat to this treat. Not for the faint of heart.

2	*tablespoons vegetable oil*
3	*lbs. lean stew beef, cut into 1/2-inch cubes*
1	*lb pork loin, cut into 1/2-inch cubes*
3	*large onions, finely chopped*
1	*tablespoon ground cumin*
7	*garlic cloves*
1	*tablespoon ground New Mexico red chile*
1	*teaspoon Tabasco sauce*
2	*teaspoons salt*
10	*jalapeño peppers, seeded, deveined*
1	*lb. fresh or canned tomatoes*
	sugar to taste
1	*(12-oz.) can beer*
1	*oz. unsweetened chocolate*
4	*cups water*
1/2	*cup masa harina*
1/2	*cup cold water*

1. In a large Dutch oven or a heavy pot, heat oil over medium heat. Brown meat. Add onions and cook until soft.

2. In a blender or food processor, blend cumin, garlic, ground chiles, Tabasco, salt, jalapeños and tomatoes. Add to meat and onions.

3. Add sugar, beer and chocolate to mixture; simmer uncovered, 2 hours, stirring occasionally. Add water as necessary to keep chili soupy.

4. One half hour before serving, mix masa with 1/2 cup cold water to make a paste and add to chili. Stir briskly and thicken chili.

5. During the last half hour of cooking, stir frequently to avoid sticking. Add salt to taste.

Makes 12 servings.

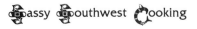

NEVER FAIL CHILI

For a novice this is a great way to start cooking chili. Easy and foolproof. You can't miss with this one.

2	*teaspoons vegetable oil*
1-1/2	*lbs. ground beef*
1	*(28-oz.) can stewed tomatoes, cored and chopped (Reserve 1 cup liquid)*
1	*medium yellow onion, chopped*
1	*(23-oz.) can ranch style beans*
2	*tablespoons red chili powder*
1	*teaspoon ground cumin*
1	*teaspoon brown sugar*
2	*teaspoons salt*
1/2	*teaspoon garlic powder*
3	*cups water*

1. In a large 4-quart Dutch oven or heavy pot, heat oil; add beef, cook until brown, stirring frequently. Drain and discard liquid.

2. Add remaining ingredients plus reserved tomato juice. Mix thoroughly and add enough water to make desired consistency. Place on low heat and simmer uncovered for 1 hour.

Makes 6 servings.

In New Mexico. there is an unwritten law that no cowboy can ride his horse on the windward side of the chuckwagon fire in a cow camp. The rule is observed so that no trash or dirt will be stirred up and blown into the kettles or skillets. The chuckwagon cook (known as a Cosi) will run off any green hand who violates this serious breach of manners.

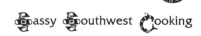

NUMEX BIG JIM CHILI

The use of chocolate in chili is one of Old Mexico's influence on our cooking. Add beans and you have a chili that is definitely different. Try it--you'll like it.

2	*tablespoons vegetable oil*
1	*medium white onion, finely chopped*
2	*garlic cloves, minced*
1	*lb. lean beef, coarse ground*
1/2	*cup water*
1	*(16-oz.) can kidney beans, drained*
1	*(16-oz.) can tomato puree*
1	*(6-oz.) can tomato paste*
8	*Green NuMex Big Jim chiles, roasted, peeled, seeded, deveined and chopped, or 2 (8-oz.) cans chopped green chiles*
1	*beef bouillon cube*
1	*teaspoon ground cumin*
2	*(1-oz.) pieces bittersweet chocolate salt and fresh ground black pepper to taste*

1. In a large Dutch oven or heavy pot, heat oil. Add onion and garlic cook until onion is soft.

2. Add meat to the pot. Cook, breaking up with fork, stirring frequently, until meat is brown.

3. Combine water with kidney beans, tomato puree, tomato paste, green chiles, beef bouillon, cumin and 1 oz. of chocolate. Mix well. Bring to a rolling boil; reduce heat and simmer uncovered, for 1/2 hour. Stir occasionally.

4. Stir in remaining chocolate and continue cooking until thoroughly blended. Season with salt and pepper to taste.

Makes 2 servings.

GREEN PICANTE CHILI

Choose your favorite picante sauce for this easy to prepare dish.

1   *tablespoon olive oil*
2   *lbs. lean pork, cut into 1/2-inch cubes*
2   *red bell peppers, seeded and chopped*
2   *white onions, chopped*
2   *New Mexico chiles, roasted, peeled, seeded,*
       deveined and chopped
2   *jalapeño chiles, seeded and chopped*
1   *cup water*
1   *(16-oz.) jar green Picante sauce*
3   *tablespoons all-purpose flour*
1/2   *cup water*

1. In a large Dutch oven or heavy pot, heat oil; add pork cubes a few at a time, stirring to brown evenly.

2. Add chopped vegetables. Cover with water and simmer uncovered for 1 hour, stirring occasionally.

3. Pour in picante sauce; simmer for 45 minutes to one hour, until meat is tender.

4. Blend flour and water together to make a smooth paste. Stir into chili mixture and cook for 10 to 15 minutes on low heat.

Makes 6 servings.

Early in September the Hatch Chile Festival is held in Hatch, New Mexico. There is a theme parade, sassy food, drinks and prizes for the biggest and best chile.

TWO-BEAN CHILI

Not all chili requires long cooking. This one is ready in minutes.

1/2	*lb. chorizo sausage*
1	*medium white onion, chopped*
1	*(14.5-oz.) can beef broth*
2	*(15.5-oz.) cans red beans, drained and rinsed*
1	*(15.5-oz.) can pinto beans, drained and rinsed*
2	*(15.5-oz.) cans tomato sauce*
2	*(4-oz.) cans New Mexico chiles, chopped*
1	*tablespoon chili powder*
3	*teaspoons ground cumin*
1/4	*teaspoon salt*
1/4	*teaspoon fresh ground black pepper*
1/8	*teaspoon cayenne pepper*

1. Remove the casing from chorizo sausage; discard. Crumble sausage.

2. In large Dutch oven or heavy pot, cook sausage and onion until onion is soft. Add remaining ingredients; mix well. Cook 10 to 15 minutes or until thoroughly heated, stirring occasionally.

Makes 6 to 8 servings.

TURKEY CHILI WITH ANASAZI BEANS

A new way to use up left over turkey. It is accompanied by my favorite bean, the Anasazi.

1	*lb. dry Anasazi beans*
6	*cups distilled water*
3	*tablespoons olive oil*
1	*white onion, minced*
3	*cloves garlic, minced*
2	*(4-oz.) cans New Mexico green chile chopped*
1	*tablespoon ground cumin*
1	*tablespoon dried-leaf oregano*
1	*teaspoon ground cinnamon*
1	*pinch cayenne pepper*
3	*cups chicken broth*
4	*cups cooked turkey, cut into 1-inch pieces*
1-1/2	*cup shredded Monterey Jack cheese*
	salt
	fresh ground black pepper to taste
	salsa of choice for garnish
	sour cream for garnish
	minced cilantro for garnish

1. Rinse beans and place in kettle with water. Cook about 45 minutes until beans are tender. Drain and set aside.

2. In a large Dutch oven or heavy pot, heat oil; add onion and garlic and cook until soft.

3. Add chiles, cumin, oregano, cinnamon, and cayenne pepper; cook 3 minutes.

4. Add beans and chicken broth. Bring to boil and reduce heat. Cover and simmer about 2 hours until beans are tender, stirring occasionally.

5. Stir in turkey. Season to taste with salt and pepper. Just before serving, stir in cheese. Heat 1 to 2 minutes until cheese is melted.

Makes 6 servings.

Sassy Southwest Cooking

WILD GAME

When cooking wild game it's important to remember that the end results are always determined by the quality of the meat you start with. When you begin with meat of an aged animal don't expect a tender roast. Hunting for trophies and hunting for food should be considered two different things. When all expenses are considered, the cost per pound of wild game far exceeds the cost of other meats. It only makes sense to be sure that it is properly cleaned and cared for before returning home with the meat.

On the homestead we ate a lot of venison. Cattle were a cash crop and venison was available year round, in spite of what the game warden thought.

Wild meat is tougher and leaner and needs aging. All game meat should be properly aged. For best results meat or birds should be at 40F(5C) dry cold if possible. Here is an approximate time table. Wild duck and goose, 6 to 8 days; pheasant, 8 to 10 days; rabbit, 2 to 3 days; wild turkey, 6 days; venison, 10 days to 3 weeks. Some meats require further tenderizing—usually accomplished by marinating.

It is sometimes necessary to add fats in the cooking. The recipes I feature here are best when used with aged meat. Eating wild game can be a coveted experience; it should never be wasted because of poor preparation.

ANTELOPE BARBECUE

I know of no better way to prepare the meat of the West's swiftest animal.

3   lb. aged antelope steaks
Salt pork or oil
1   cup catsup
1   tablespoon salt
3   slices fresh lemon
1   white onion, thinly sliced
1/3   cup prepared steak sauce
2   tablespoons tarragon vinegar
1   tablespoon red chili powder

1. Preheat oven to 350F(175C).

2. In a large skillet, sear antelope steaks with slices of salt pork or oil.

3. In large Dutch oven or heavy pot. Add remaining ingredients and bring to boil. Stirring occasionally.

4. Add steaks, turn to cover with sauce. Bake about 1 1/2 hours, turning occasionally.

Makes 4 servings.

New Mexico's Bureau of Land Management oversees approximately 13-million acres of public land, which offers a full range of excellent big game hunting. Also available are unusual recreational opportunities. These include ski slopes and water activities like the Wild Rivers Recreational Area (35 miles north of Taos).

BAKED RAINBOW TROUT

I also like trout rubbed with butter, a little salt and grilled in aluminum foil.

6	**rainbow trout**
2	**teaspoons salt**
2/3	**cup butter**
4	**cups soft bread cubes**
1	**cup fresh mushrooms, sliced**
2/3	**cup green onions, sliced**
1/4	**cup fresh parsley, chopped**
2	**tablespoons pimento, chopped**
4	**tablespoons lemon juice**
1/2	**teaspoon dried-marjoram leaves**

1. Preheat oven to 375F(175C) and grease a baking dish.

2. Clean, wash and dry trout. Sprinkle 1 1/2 teaspoons salt evenly inside and outside of fish.

3. In a medium skillet, heat 1/2 cup butter and saute bread until lightly browned, stirring frequently. Add mushrooms and onions. Cook until tender. Stir in remaining salt, parsley, pimento, lemon juice and marjoram; toss lightly. Cool.

4. Stuff each trout with mixture. Place in a single layer in prepared baking dish. Brush with remaining melted butter.

5. Bake for 15 to 20 minutes or until fish flakes easily.

Makes 6 servings.

BAKED PHEASANT & RICE

Pheasant over rice, what a way to enjoy the most beautiful of our game birds.

2	*pheasants, cleaned*
1	*(10-oz.) can condensed cream of mushroom soup*
2/3	*cup milk*
3/4	*cup long grain rice, uncooked*
1/2	*cup sliced fresh mushrooms or 1 (4-oz.) can mushrooms, undrained*
1	*(1.5-oz.) pkg. dehydrated onion soup*
2	*tablespoons melted butter*
	Paprika

1. Cut pheasant into serving pieces.

2. Preheat oven to 325F(165C).

3. In a small bowl, blend mushroom soup, milk, rice, mushrooms with juice, and onion soup mix.

4. Pour mixture into a 13 x 9 x 2 baking dish. Arrange pheasant pieces on top. Brush with melted butter, sprinkle with paprika.

5. Bake uncovered for 1-1/2 hours.

Makes 6 servings.

BRAISED RABBIT

As a young man, I raised and ate a lot of rabbits. Today we have commercial production of rabbit and you can find it in the freezer section of your supermarket.

1	*young rabbit, cleaned and skinned*
1	*cup all-purpose flour*
2	*teaspoons salt, divided*
1/4	*teaspoon ground red New Mexico chile, divided*
6	*tablespoons shortening*
1	*cup chicken broth*
3	*tablespoons lemon juice*
6	*tablespoons orange juice*
1	*small white onion, chopped*
1	*dash ginger*
1	*cup fresh mushrooms, sliced*

1. Cut rabbit into serving pieces. In a bowl combine flour, 1 teaspoon salt and 1/8 teaspoon red chile.

2. Dredge rabbit in flour mixture. Heat shortening in large skillet, saute until brown. Reduce heat and drain off excess fat.

3. Add broth, lemon and orange juices, and onion. Season with remaining salt, red chile, and ginger. Cover and simmer about 1-hour until tender. Add mushrooms during last 15 minutes of cooking. If desired, thicken juices with seasoned flour.

Makes 4 servings.

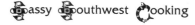

BUFFALO TONGUE

You will be pleasantly surprised with this unusual dish. Thinly slice and use for sandwiches.

1	*buffalo or cow tongue*
4	*bay leaves*
1/2	*teaspoon black peppercorns*
1	*white onion, chopped*
1	*Madeira Sauce (page 130)*

1. In a large saucepan, cover tongue with water. Bring to boil. Reduce heat; add bay leaves, peppercorns and onion. Cover and simmer for 3 to 4 hours until tongue is soft. Add water as necessary. Cool.

2. With a sharp knife, remove and discard skin. Cut meat into 1/2-inch thick pieces. Serve warm or cold. Serve with Madeira Sauce.

 American buffalo is now being raised commercially. This wonderful animal is really a bison, a shaggy humped member of the cattle family. The tongue is the most valued of all buffalo meat. The meat is very tender and tastes a lot like lean beef. It doesn't have a strong-gamey flavor. Here in New Mexico, media mogul Ted Turner owns the Ladder Ranch and part of the old Armendariz Spanish land grants. He purchased them for raising buffalo and has the largest herd in the state. In all of New Mexico, there are an estimated 5,000 to 6,000 buffalo.

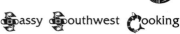

BURGUNDY VENISON STEAK TIPS

The best of the best. You must try venison in a rich deep colored sauce.

3	*tablespoons oil*
2	*lbs. venison steak, cut in small cubes*
2 to 3	*tablespoons dry onion soup mix*
3	*beef-bouillon cubes*
2	*cups water*
1	*cup Burgundy wine*
1	*cup fresh mushrooms or 1 (4-oz.) can, drained*
3	*cups cooked rice*

1. In large Dutch oven or heavy pot, heat oil and brown venison.

2. Add remaining ingredients except mushrooms and rice. Cover and simmer for about one hour.

3. Add mushrooms the last 5 minutes.

4. Serve over rice.

Makes 6 servings.

Deer meat is much like beef, except the lean part is sweeter and the fat has a much stronger taste. Although New Mexicans generally are referring to deer meat when they use the term venison, venison refers to the meat of deer, elk, reindeer, antelope, moose, or any large antlered animal.

CHEROKEE VENISON MEATLOAF

Most butchers end up with a lot of ground venison when they cut up your game. I like to use some of it for this meatloaf.

1/2	*cup cornmeal*
1/2	*cup water*
2	*tablespoons oil*
1	*lb. ground venison*
2	*tablespoons oil of choice*
1	*(17-oz.) can whole kernel corn, drained*
1	*small yellow onion, chopped*
1	*teaspoon salt*
2	*eggs*
	Madeira Sauce, (page 130)
	Spanish Rice, page (page 94)

1. Place cornmeal in a small bowl, add water and blend. Set aside.

2. In skillet heat oil, cook venison until brown. Add corn and onion. Cook 10 minutes. Add salt, egg and cornmeal. Thoroughly combine. Cook 15 minutes longer.

3. Preheat oven to 350F(175C) and grease a loaf pan.

4. Spoon mixture into prepared pan. Bake 35 to 45 minutes. Serve with Madeira Sauce and Spanish Rice.

Makes 8 servings.

Venison's natural flavor is sweeter than beef. Tomato sauce, unsweetened berry sauce, vinegar and French dressing compliment its rich flavor. Do not overcook, it's short fibers toughen quickly if it is overcooked or at too high a temperature. Venison is best when it is medium to well done; never serve it rare or overdone.

CRAYFISH QUICHE

If you haven't eaten crawdads otherwise know as crayfish you have missed out. Long overlooked, this is a delicate dish you will remember.

48	*live crayfish*
6	*peppercorns*
1	*bay leaf*
4	*eggs*
1	*cup celery, diced*
1	*cup Cheddar cheese, grated*
1-1/2	*cups mayonnaise*
1-1/2	*tablespoons Worcestershire sauce*
3	*tablespoons sherry*
1	*cup buttered bread crumbs*

1. Preheat oven to 325F(165C) and butter a medium baking dish.

2. Rinse crayfish in clean water or soak them for 24 hours in fresh water. Discard any that are dead before cooking.

3. Heat a large pot of water to boiling, add peppercorns and bay leaf. Drop in crayfish and boil 6 to 10 minutes until bright red. Cool and shell. Chop meat.

3. In a bowl, beat eggs until frothy. Add crayfish and remaining ingredients except bread crumbs.

4. Pour mixture into prepared dish and top with bread crumbs; bake for one hour. Can be served warm or refrigerated for later use.

Makes 8 servings.

Crawdads, or crayfish, can be found in most shallow unpolluted water. They are caught with traps or a baited line or by hand. They are often used as bait. To transport, place them in a bucket of cool water. A dozen will feed one person.

DUCK WITH ORANGE

My dad always told me if you shoot it you better eat it. Duck was a real problem for me until I found this recipe.

2	*(5 lb.) ducks, cleaned and plucked*
2	*cups water*
1	*white onion, quartered*
1/4	*teaspoon dried-thyme leaves*
1/2	*bay leaf*
5	*teaspoons salt*
1/2	*teaspoon fresh ground black pepper*
3	*oranges*
1/2	*cup white wine*
	all-purpose flour

1. In a saucepan cook giblets, necks, and wing tips with water, onion, thyme, bay leaf and 1 teaspoon of salt. Simmer for 45 minutes.

2. Preheat oven to 450F(230C).

3. Meanwhile, rub each duck with 1 teaspoon salt and 1/4 teaspoon of pepper. Cut 1 orange into 8 pieces, place 4 pieces in the cavity of each duck. Place ducks in a baking dish, prick duck breasts, roast uncovered 20 minutes.

4. Slice 1 orange very thin, set aside. Shred peel from remaining orange and then juice.

5. Prick ducks many times again and pour off fat. Cover with orange slices. Reduce oven temperature to 350F(175C).

6. In a small bowl, combine wine, orange juice and remaining salt. Pour over ducks, cook for 1 hour. Baste every 10 minutes, turning the birds to brown evenly. If not brown enough, increase temperature to 450F(230C) and bake 10 minutes longer.

6. Place the ducks on a serving platter and keep warm. Skim fat from the baking dish juices. Add orange peel and 1 cup of strained broth from giblets. Thicken with flour and water paste. Serve as sauce.

Makes 6-8 servings.

Sassy Southwest Cooking

QUAIL IN CABBAGE LEAVES

These little birds dry out so quickly that it is very difficult to fix them and keep their delicate flavor. This old trick works well, wrapped in the cabbage leaves, they hold their moisture and the spices enhance their wonderful taste.

4	*dressed quail*
	salt and fresh ground black pepper
4	*cups shredded cabbage*
4	*slices cooked bacon, crumbled*
16	*large cabbage leaves*
2	*tablespoons butter*
1	*cup chicken stock*
4	*small apples, sliced*
1/4	*teaspoon dried-thyme leaves, crushed*
1/4	*teaspoon dried-tarragon leaves, crushed*
1/4	*teaspoon caraway seeds, crushed*
1	*teaspoon salt*
1/4	*teaspoon fresh ground black pepper*

1. Sprinkle quail with salt and pepper.

2. In a small bowl, combine shredded cabbage and bacon. Place stuffing in each bird. Wrap each in 4 cabbage leaves; tie with string. Set aside.

3. Place remaining ingredients in saucepan, simmer 5 minutes.

4. Place birds in large Dutch oven or heavy pot, pour saucepan mixture over birds. Bring to a boil; reduce heat, cover and simmer 20 to 25 minutes until tender. Remove string and cabbage leaves and serve with the sauce.

Makes 4 servings.

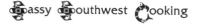

ROAST GOOSE

When you are lucky enough to get a goose, you will want to celebrate and this is a good way to reward yourself. Or you can purchase a frozen goose at the market.

    1   *goose, (4 to 7 lbs.) cleaned and dried*
    2   *teaspoons salt*
  1/2   *teaspoon fresh ground black pepper*

Stuffing Mix:
  10   *small new-red potatoes peeled, quartered*
    1   *cup onions, chopped*
  1/4   *teaspoon fresh ground black pepper*
  1/2   *pound salt pork*
    1   *teaspoon poultry seasoning*
    1   *tablespoon oil*
  1/2   *cup celery, chopped*
    4   *slices dry bread, crumbed*
    2   *eggs, beaten*
    1   *teaspoon salt*

1. Clean and dry goose, rub inside and out with salt and pepper.

2. In a pan boil potatoes in water to cover. Remove from water and quarter. Reserve potato water for basting.

3. In large skillet, heat oil and saute onion and celery. Add remaining stuffing ingredients, mix and cool.

4. Stuff goose with mixture and bake 300F(155C) 3-4 hours, basting from time to time with reserved potato water.

Makes 4 servings.

ROAST VENISON

A wine marinade serves a two-fold purpose, it adds a robust flavor as well as tenderizing the roast.

2	*cups Burgundy wine*
1	*cup beef bouillon*
1	*onion, sliced*
1	*clove garlic, crushed*
1	*bay leaf*
1	*(6 to 7 lb.) boneless leg of venison*
1	*teaspoon salt*
6	*slices fat salt pork*

1. In a large bowl combine, wine, beef bouillon, onion and garlic, bay leaf and venison. Cover and refrigerate for 24 hours.

2. Remove meat from marinade, skewer and tie into a roll. Strain marinade and reserve. If meat thermometer is used, insert it in the thickest part.

3. Preheat oven to 450F(230C). Place meat on a rack in a shallow roasting pan. Place salt pork slices on top of meat. Roast, uncovered, for 20 minutes. Reduce heat to 325F(165C) and cook 15 to 18 minutes per lb. or to an internal temperature to 140F(60C) for very rare, 150F(65C) for medium to well done. Baste occasionally with marinade.

4. Transfer meat to heated serving platter. Remove and discard fat from pan drippings. Strain and serve as sauce.

Makes 8 to 10 servings.

VENISON AU VIN

Hunters are always looking for a way to use stew meat. Pairing with fresh mushrooms and wild rice makes this dish an extra special treat.

1/4	*lb. salt pork*
1	*lb. venison stew meat*
1/2	*cup all-purpose flour*
1	*cup white wine*
1/2	*teaspoon salt*
1/2	*teaspoon fresh ground black pepper*
1	*small bay leaf*
1	*teaspoon parsley flakes*
2	*white onions, quartered*
2	*cups potatoes, peeled, diced*
3	*tomatoes, chopped*
2	*cups fresh mushrooms*
3	*cups cooked wild rice*

1. In a large skillet, fry salt pork until crisp. Remove meat. Coat venison with flour and brown in hot skillet.

2. In a large Dutch over or heavy pot, add wine, salt, pepper, bay leaf and parsley. Bring to a simmer; add venison, onions, potatoes, tomatoes and mushrooms.

3. Cover and bake at 350F(175C) for about 3 hours. Add wine if needed, to keep moist. Serve over wild rice.

Makes 6 servings.

Sassy Southwest Cooking

VENISON JERKY

One of the many rewards for a successful hunt is venison jerky.

> **4**   *lbs. venison flank steak, partially frozen*
> **6**   *tablespoon water*
> **6**   *tablespoons Worcestershire sauce*
> **3**   *teaspoons salt*
> **6**   *garlic cloves, minced*
> **1/4**   *teaspoon ground red chile*
> **3**   *teaspoons ground cumin*
> **4**   *teaspoons chili powder*

1. Trim off all the fat. Slice meat cross grain into long 1/8-inch strips 1-inch wide.

2. In a large bowl, whisk together water, Worcestershire, salt, garlic, ground red chile, cumin and chili powder. Add meat strips and coat thoroughly. Tightly cover and marinate 6 hours or overnight.

3. Remove meat and pat with paper towel to remove any excess liquid.

4. Preheat oven to 200F(95C). Place strips on racks in a foil-lined 9 x 13 baking dishes. About 6 rack and dishes will be required. Bake about 5 to 6 hours until meat feels dry to touch and is dark brown. Allow room for air to circulate around dishes. Pat with toweling to remove beads of oil. Cool and store in airtight container in refrigerator.

5. Or for dehydrator, place strips in a single layer, on a dryer rack. Follow manufacturers' instructions for time and temperature.

Makes 15 to 18 oz.

During the settling of the American West, Jerky was simply sun- dried lean meat. Today, packaged jerky is not the same as genuine Jerky. Most of today's is a pressed by-product made from meat scraps which have been pickled, baked and coated with a smoke flavoring. Homemade jerky made from venison is virtually fat free and superior to beef jerky.

WILD GAME MINCEMEAT

Most mincemeats today do not contain meat. Old recipes like this did. Use as filling for pies, tarts, puddings and cookies.

2-1/2	*lbs. venison stew meat*
1	*lb. beef suet, chopped*
1/2	*lb. dried currants*
2	*lbs. seedless dark raisins*
5	*lbs. tart apples, coarsely chopped*
1/2	*tablespoon cinnamon*
1/2	*teaspoon ground allspice*
1	*teaspoon ground cloves*
1/2	*teaspoon freshly ground black pepper*
2	*teaspoons salt*
2/3	*cup apple jelly*
2/3	*cup red currant jelly*
2	*(16-oz) cans tart cherries, undrained*
4	*cups apple cider*
3/4	*cup apple cider vinegar*

1. In sauce pan, cover venison with water and bring to a boil. Reduce heat and simmer until tender. Drain and process in food processor until finely chopped.

2. In a non-reactive saucepan combine remaining ingredients and bring to a boil stirring frequently. Add venison and boil for 30 minutes, stirring frequently. Cool quickly; pack into freezer containers. This mincemeat can be frozen for up to 4 months.

Makes 8 to 10 cups.

One recipe makes enough for 3 pies. Add 3 tablespoons of brandy to the filling for each pie. Bake double-crusted pies at 425F(220C) about 40 minutes or until crust is browned and filling is bubbly.

SAUCES

Without sauces, many New Mexican dishes would be bland and without soul. Cooked sauces that judiciously use chiles, red or green, are the heart of New Mexico cuisine. Knowledge of chiles and their characteristics determines the quality of the sauces you prepare. This vegetable has a range of color, heat, and taste that can enhance any dish if properly prepared.

Green chile sauces are more perishable than red and should be prepared fresh when used. Red chile sauces made from dried red chile pods or ground red chile will keep for a longer period of time if refrigerated. In selecting chile for sauces look for brightly colored, blemish free pods. Ground chile has a short life. After the container is opened, store unused portion in the refrigerator. Whenever possible use freshly ground chile or chili powder.

I have tried to give you a nice selection of sauces. They represent a broad range of tastes. Also included are my favorite best wild game sauces.

GREEN CHILE SAUCE

One of the two basic sauces that are necessary to New Mexico cooking. I particularly like this version. Green sauce should have a clear, sharper taste than red.

2	*tablespoons olive oil*
1/4	*cup white onion, finely chopped*
1	*garlic clove, finely minced*
2	*tablespoons all purpose flour*
1/2	*teaspoon ground cumin*
1-1/2	*cups chicken broth*
1-1/2	*cups green New Mexico chiles, roasted, peeled, seeded, deveined and chopped*
1/4	*teaspoon dried-leaf oregano*
1	*tablespoon jalapeño chile, seeded and chopped*
	salt to taste

1. In a 3-quart saucepan, heat oil; saute and stir onion and garlic. Whisk in flour and cumin. When mixture begins to brown, remove it from heat.

2. Whisking constantly, slowly stir in broth. Add green chiles and oregano. Return to heat.

3. Bring to simmer, stirring frequently. Cover and cook about 10 minutes.

4. Add jalapeño and salt to taste. If a smooth texture is desired puree in food blender.

Makes 2 cups.

Sassy Southwest Cooking

HOT TOMATO SAUCE

A versatile sauce that can be used in a number of dishes. You can easily control the heat by increasing or decreasing the amount of Jalapeño peppers you use.

2	***lbs. ripe tomatoes***
2	***tablespoons olive oil***
1/2	***cup white onion, chopped***
1	***garlic clove, minced***
1	***jalapeño chile, seeded and chopped***
1	***teaspoon fresh chopped oregano leaves***
	salt to taste
	fresh ground black pepper

1. Rinse tomatoes and core them. Cut in half crosswise; place skin side up on a rack in a roasting pan.

2. Broil 4 to 5 inches from heat until tomatoes are completely blackened. Cool and remove skin, set aside.

3. In a medium skillet, heat oil. Cook onions and garlic until soft. Add tomatoes, oregano and jalapeño pepper.

4. Cook over medium heat for 15 minutes. Cool and place in blender or food processor puree. Season to taste with salt and pepper.

Makes 3-1/2 cups.

MADEIRA SAUCE

Serve this rich sauce with all kinds of meats. Use Bual or Verdelho a medium-sweet variety of Madeira.

1/2	*cup golden raisins*
1/4	*cup butter*
1	*tablespoon white onion, minced*
3	*tablespoons all-purpose flour*
2	*cups canned condensed consomme, undiluted*
1/3	*cup Madeira wine*
	pinch of cayenne pepper

1. Soak raisins 10 minutes in hot water, drain and set aside.

2. In a saucepan, heat butter. Cook onion until golden brown, stirring often.

3. Sprinkle flour over onions and continue to stir about 3 minutes until blended. Be careful not to scorch the flour.

4. Stir in consomme and continue stirring until mixture thickens.

5. Add raisins, madeira and cayenne. Cook for 1 to 2 minutes. Do not boil. Serve hot.

Makes about 2-1/2 cups.

American-made Madeira is not as distinctive as the Portuguese or Spanish wines but costs a fraction of the price of the imports.

MOLE SAUCE

Often called the "National Dish of Mexico", mole pronounced "mo-lay", has always been popular here in New Mexico. Taste the subtle blend of chocolate and chile.

2	*corn tortillas, slightly dried*
1	*(1-oz.) square unsweetened chocolate*
1	*garlic clove, chopped*
1/4	*cup blanched almonds*
1	*small white onion, chopped*
2	*tablespoons seedless raisins*
3	*New Mexico green chiles, roasted, seeded, deveined and chopped, or 1 (4-oz.) can green chiles chopped*
1	*large tomato, quartered*
3	*tablespoons all-purpose flour*
1	*teaspoon ground red chile*
1/4	*teaspoon ground cinnamon*
1/4	*teaspoon ground, cloves*
2-1/2	*cups chicken stock*

1. Tear tortillas into pieces.

2. In a food processor or blender, add tortillas pieces, chocolate, garlic, almonds, onion, raisins, chiles and tomato; cover and process to a rough puree.

3. Pour into a 3-quart saucepan; stir in flour and spices. Add chicken stock and blend. Bring to a boil; reduce heat. Simmer uncovered, for 20 minutes, stirring occasionally. The sauce should be the consistency of heavy cream.

Makes 2-1/2 cups.

PECOS VALLEY BARBECUE SAUCE

The moderate temperature and long pleasant evenings in New Mexico encourage outdoor barbecuing. We also have some of the finest beef available anywhere. This sauce comes from the Pecos Valley.

4	*tablespoons butter*
1	*small white onion, chopped*
4	*garlic cloves, chopped*
2	*(4-oz.) cans New Mexico green chiles, chopped*
1	*teaspoon ground paprika*
1	*tablespoon ground black pepper*
1/4	*cup fresh lemon juice*
1	*teaspoon dry mustard*
1/2	*teaspoon ground red chile*
1/2	*teaspoon salt*
1/4	*cup vinegar*
1	*(16-oz.) can tomato sauce*

1. In medium saucepan heat butter, add onions and garlic. Cook until onions are soft.

2. Stir in next 7 ingredients; cook over medium heat about 5 minutes. Add vinegar and tomato sauce; bring to boil.

3. Reduce heat and simmer uncovered about 15 minutes until sauce thickens slightly.

Makes 2 to 2-1/2 cups.

 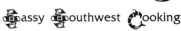

PIQUANT PLUM SAUCE

Appealingly provocative, this sauce is a good way for you to fully appreciate the term piquant. An unusual taste treat you must try.

4	*tablespoons sesame oil*
3	*tablespoons fresh ginger, minced*
2	*garlic cloves, minced*
1/2	*cup wine vinegar*
2	*pounds ripe purple plums, pitted and halved*
4	*tablespoons lime juice*
1/2	*cup water*
2	*teaspoons red chile pepper flakes salt salt*

1. In medium sauce pan, heat oil over medium heat; add ginger and garlic and saute, stirring constantly, until golden brown about 1 minute.

2. Add remaining ingredients, simmer, 10 to 12 minutes stirring frequently until plums are cooked.

3. Cool 10 minutes, then puree in food processor or blender. Use at once or store in refrigerator for up to 3 days. Return to room temperature before serving.

Makes 4 cups.

RED CHILE SAUCE

If you can't make a good red chile sauce you can't cook New Mexican. Red and green sauces are critical to this style of cooking. Here is an easy basic one.

2	**tablespoons vegetable oil**
1	**cup white onion, finely chopped**
1	**garlic clove, minced**
1/2	**cup New Mexico ground hot red chile**
1/2	**cup New Mexico ground mild red chile**
1	**(12-oz.) can tomato sauce**
	salt to taste
6	**cups water**

1. In a 3-quart saucepan, heat oil; add onions and garlic and saute until onions are soft. Do not brown.

2. Stir in chile powders, tomato sauce and water. Simmer uncovered until sauce desired consistency. Season lightly with salt.

3. Sauce may be used as is or pureed. Refrigerate in tightly-covered container or may be frozen.

Makes about 5 cups.

ROASTED NEW MEXICO CHILE CREAM SAUCE

Another example of why our New Mexican cuisine is gaining in popularity.

> 3 *New Mexico chiles, roasted, peeled, seeded, deveined and chopped*
> 3 *Serrano chiles, seeded and chopped*
> 4 *shallots, minced*
> 3 *garlic cloves, minced*
> 2 *cups chicken stock*
> 2 *cups heavy whipping cream*
> 3/4 *cup fresh cilantro, chopped*
> 4 *medium sorrel leaves, chopped*
> *lemon juice and salt*
> *cooked pasta*
> 1/2 *cup Parmesan cheese, grated*
> 1/4 *cup piñon nuts, roasted*

1. In a saucepan combine the New Mexico chiles, Serrano chiles, shallots, garlic, stock and whipping cream in saucepan.

2. Bring to a boil, lower heat and simmer until liquid is reduced by half.

3. Pour into food processor or blender. Add cilantro and sorrel leaves and process until smooth. Strain through a fine sieve. Season to taste with lemon juice and salt.

4. Pour over pasta, toss with Parmesan cheese and top with piñon nuts.

Makes 2-1/2 cups.

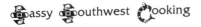

SAN JUAN BARBECUE SAUCE

Barbecue aficionados will appreciate this sauce. Molasses and Liquid Smoke are the keys to any great sauce.

1	*tablespoon oil*
1/2	*cup yellow onion, finely chopped*
1	*garlic clove, minced*
1	*(14-oz.) bottle ketchup*
1	*teaspoon Liquid Smoke*
6	*tablespoons Worcestershire sauce*
1/4	*cup red wine vinegar*
2	*tablespoons molasses*
1	*teaspoon dry mustard*
1/8	*cup ground red chile*
3/4	*teaspoon cumin*

1. In a 3-quart saucepan, heat oil; cook and stir onions and garlic until soft.

2. Add remaining ingredients. Simmer uncovered for 15 minutes, stirring occasionally.

Makes 3 cups.

  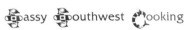

THREE CHILE SAUCE

Fiery is the only way to describe this sauce. Not for amateurs, not for the faint of heart. If you have been looking for a sauce with heat, this one is for you.

4	*dried ancho chiles*
1	*chipotle chile*
4	*dried casabel chiles*
3	*cups boiling water*
1/4	*cup oil*
3	*garlic cloves, chopped*
1	*small white onion, diced*
1	*tablespoon cumin seeds*
1	*tablespoon dried-leaf oregano*
	salt to taste

1. In a bowl, cover the chiles with boiling water. Let stand for 30 minutes or until softened.

2. Strain chiles and reserve liquid. Remove stems and devein.

3. Heat oil in a 2-quart saucepan. Add garlic and onion; stir until onion is tender. Stir in chiles, reserved liquid and remaining ingredients.

4. Heat to boiling; reduce heat. Simmer uncovered 20 minutes; cool.

5. Pour into a food processor or blender; cover and puree. Rub puree through a fine strainer and discard residue. Cover and refrigerate for up to 10 days.

Makes 2 cups.

TOMATILLO CHILE SAUCE

The development of sauces like this one will keep our style of cooking in the forefront of American cuisine for years to come.

1/2	*lb. fresh tomatillos or 2 (13-oz.) cans, drained*
1	*jalapeño chile, seeded*
2	*tablespoons fresh cilantro, chopped*
1/2	*small white onion, chopped*
1	*garlic clove, chopped*
1-1/2	*teaspoons oil*
1/2	*cup chicken stock*
	Salt to taste

1. Remove husks from tomatillos and chop. Color should be bright-green, not yellow.

2. In small saucepan, place tomatillos and chiles, add water to cover. Bring to a boil; reduce heat and simmer about 10 minutes until tender.

3. Remove tomatillos and chiles with slotted spoon and cool.

4. In a food processor or blender, place all ingredients except chicken stock, and pulse to a coarse puree.

5. Heat oil in medium skillet. Add puree and cook, stirring constantly about 5 minutes until mixture darkens and thickens.

6. Add chicken broth; bring to boil, reduce heat and simmer until the mixture thickens slightly. Season with salt to taste. Serve warm.

Makes 4 servings.

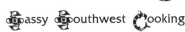

SALSA

Salsa is one of the food sensations of the 90's. The endless variety is making it a part of every cooks presentations. Elusively simple in appearance yet complex in composition, salsa is now outselling ketchup, proof that it is becoming America's favorite condiment. The fusion of spice, texture and flavors has brought this New Mexican original to the forefront. Salsa is used as an appetizer, side dish or dessert.

Sassy or sweet, this taste sensation is only as good as the ingredients you use. Take advantage of the seasons and utilize fruits and vegetables at their peak. Salsa provides you with the chance to experiment and be creative, but be careful—it is easier to make hot salsa than it is to eat it.

This group of salsas represents a wide variety of flavors and textures. Use these as a base and adjust the ingredients to suit your taste. A blender or food processor is essential in the successful preparation of a good salsa. Remember that a great salsa must include an element from at least three of the following categories: spicy/hot, sour/tart, savory, herbal, sweet, or aromatic. This will give you the excitement and taste titillation that has made salsa number one.

APRICOT JICAMA SALSA

I like to use the jicama because of its slightly sweet, crisp texture. It is a great offset for soft fruit and holds its own with all kinds of fruits and vegetables.

1	*medium jicama*
4	*apricots, pitted and cut into 1/2-inch strips*
2	*tablespoons fresh cilantro, minced*
1/2	*small red onion, halved and thinly sliced*
1/2	*small red bell pepper, seeded, thinly sliced*
1	*tablespoon dried chipotle chiles, minced*
2	*tablespoons fresh lime juice*
1	*tablespoon olive oil*
	salt and fresh ground black pepper to taste

1. Using a sharp knife, remove thick outer peel of jicama.

2. Rinse in cold water and cut into matchstick pieces.

3. In a large plastic or glass bowl, place all ingredients and toss lightly. Refrigerate until ready to serve.

Makes 4 cups.

BLACKENED TOMATO-MINT SALSA

I use a dry skillet to scorch the tomato skins. This creates a smoky undertone without the use of oil. Fresh mint adds a nice touch. Mint is an easy herb to grow in pots or the open ground.

4	*medium ripe tomatoes*
1	*garlic clove*
2	*tablespoons fresh lime juice*
2	*tablespoons vegetable oil*
1/2	*teaspoon chili powder*
2	*New Mexico red chiles, roasted, peeled, seeded, deveined and finely chopped*
4	*tablespoons fresh spearmint leaves, chopped*

1. In a large non-stick skillet over high heat, blacken tomatoes by turning them frequently until the skins are scorched.

2. Remove skins and cut tomatoes in half, remove seeds and roughly chop.

3. In a food processor or blender, place tomatoes, garlic, lime juice, oil and chili powder; puree until smooth.

4. In a glass or plastic bowl, combine puree and remaining ingredients. Mix well and refrigerate until ready to serve.

Makes 2 cups.

FIESTA CORN SALSA

New Mexicans make salsa that sets the standard for all to meet. This one is especially good.

> 1   *cup water*
> 1/2   *cup fresh sweet corn kernels*
> 1   *red bell pepper seeded and chopped*
> 1/2   *cup white onion, chopped*
> 1   *clove garlic, chopped*
> 2   *yellow-wax chile peppers, peeled, seeded and deveined*
> 1/2   *cup chopped fresh cilantro*
> 1/2   *tablespoon tomato paste*
> 1/2   *cup water*
> 1/8   *teaspoon cumin*
> 1/8   *teaspoon salt*

1. In saucepan, bring water to boil. Add corn and blanch 6 to 8 seconds; drain and set aside.

2. Place bell pepper, onion, chile peppers, garlic and cilantro in a food processor. Pulse to chop, do not puree, salsa should have texture.

3. In a glass or plastic bowl, combine all ingredients. Cover and refrigerate until chilled.

4. Salsa may be stored, covered, 3 days in refrigerator.

Makes 4 servings.

FRESH BASIL SALSA

I would not know how to cook if you took away my basil. In the summer I grow it outside and in the winter in a pot in the window. Here is basil at its best.

2	*large ripe tomatoes, seeded and cut into 1/4 cubes*
1/2	*yellow onion, finely chopped*
1/4	*cup fresh basil leaves, chopped*
1	*serrano chile seeded and minced*
1	*teaspoon olive oil*
1	*teaspoon white-wine vinegar*
1/2	*teaspoon fresh lemon juice*
1/4	*teaspoon dry mustard*
1/4	*teaspoon garlic salt*
1/4	*teaspoon lemon pepper*

1. In a bowl, combine tomatoes, onion, basil and chile.

2. In a another small bowl, whisk together oil, vinegar, lemon juice and spices. Pour over vegetables and toss thoroughly. Refrigerate until served.

Makes 2 cups.

PICO DE GALLO SALSA

If you have ever eaten at a New Mexico restaurant, you have probably been served this salsa with fresh tortilla chips. A tradition I hope never changes.

2   *ripe tomatoes, seeded and chopped*
1   *small red onion, chopped*
6   *red radishes, cut chopped*
2   *serrano chiles, seeded and finely chopped*
2   *jalapeño chiles, seeded and finely chopped*
1/2   *cucumber, peeled, seeded and chopped*
1/2   *cup fresh cilantro, chopped*
1   *tablespoon fresh lime juice*
1   *tablespoon fresh lemon juice*
1   *teaspoon red-wine vinegar*
1/2   *teaspoon garlic salt*
1/2   *teaspoon lemon pepper*

1. In a glass or plastic bowl, combine tomatoes, onion, radishes, chiles, cucumber and cilantro.

2. In a small bowl, combine the remaining ingredients. Mix well.

3. Pour over vegetables and toss thoroughly. Serve immediately or cover and refrigerate. Best served freshly made.

Makes 2-1/2 cups.

Sassy Southwest Cooking

PINEAPPLE SALSA

Light and refreshing fruit salsa is a nice way to start a meal. Try your own blends of fruit and peppers. I like this combination.

2	*cups fresh pineapple, chopped*
1/2	*cup red bell pepper, seeded, chopped*
2	*tablespoons New Mexico green chiles, roasted, peeled, seeded, deveined and chopped*
2	*tablespoons green onions, chopped*
1	*tablespoon fresh cilantro, chopped*
2	*teaspoons grated fresh ginger*
1	*teaspoon grated lemon peel*
1/2	*teaspoon ground cumin*
1/4	*teaspoon salt*

1. In a glass or plastic bowl, combine all ingredients.

2. Serve at once or cover and refrigerate until chilled. Salsa may be stored, covered in refrigerator for up to 24 hours.

Makes 2-1/2 cups salsa.

PUMPKIN SEED & AVOCADO SALSA

This is one of the best uses for pumpkin seed I have found. An unusual combination of texture and tastes.

3	*tablespoons shelled pumpkin seeds, roasted*
2	*ripe avocados*
1	*serrano chile, seeded*
1	*tablespoon fresh cilantro, chopped*
1	*cup fresh parsley leaves*
1	*tablespoon fresh lemon juice*
1/4	*teaspoon salt*

1. In a large skillet, heat pumpkin seeds over medium heat. Stir constantly until toasted, about 5 minutes. Set aside to cool.

2. Cut avocados in half; remove the pits. Peel the halves and chop pulp into small chunks. Place in glass or plastic bowl.

3. In a food processor, coarsely chop pumpkin seeds, chile, cilantro and parsley. Add to avocado with lemon juice and salt. Gently mix with a fork. Serve immediately.

Makes 2 cups.

 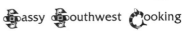

SWEET MELON-JICAMA SALSA

Crunchy jicama is blended with melons to create a sweet salsa that is contrasted by the heat of the jalapeño pepper.

1	*cup honeydew melon, peeled, seeded and chopped*
1	*cup cantaloupe melon, peeled, seeded and chopped*
1	*jalapeño chile, seeded and chopped fine*
1/2	*cup jicama, peeled and chopped*
1	*tablespoon fresh ginger, chopped fine*
2	*tablespoons fresh cilantro, chopped fine*
2	*tablespoons lime juice*

1. In a glass or plastic bowl combine all ingredients.

2. Serve at once or cover and refrigerate until chilled. Salsa may be stored, covered in refrigerator for 2 hours.

Makes 2-1/2 cups.

TOMATO SALSA

Also known as *salsa cruda*, this is one of my favorites. If you raise your own tomatoes as I do, use them to make this especially great.

6	*ripe tomatoes, chopped*
1/2	*cup white onion, chopped*
1/2	*cup green onions, chopped*
2	*garlic cloves, minced*
1	*jalapeño chile, seeded, chopped fine*
1	*tablespoon olive oil*
1	*tablespoon wine vinegar*
1/2	*cup fresh cilantro, chopped*
1	*teaspoon dried-leaf oregano*
1	*teaspoon salt*
1/2	*teaspoon fresh ground black pepper*

1. In glass or plastic bowl, combine all ingredients.

2. Cover and refrigerate for at least 4 hours before serving.

Makes 3 to 4 cups.

DESSERTS

For a traditional dish, treat yourself to Sopa Indian Bread Pudding. If you like pumpkin pie that's a little different Pecos Valley Pumpkin Pie with a butterscotch-cream sauce is one you should try. Serve it for your next party and expect compliments. An unexpected use of tortillas results in the delicious Banana and Pineapple Tortilla dessert. Rum Apple Crisp will be appreciated by both family and guests.

HONDO RAISIN CREAM PIE

Hidden under the meringue is a creamy-rich filling.

Crust:

1	*cup all-purpose flour*
1/2	*teaspoon salt*
1/3	*cup shortening*
3 to 4	*tablespoons cold water*

Cream filling:

3	*egg yolks, slightly beaten*
1-1/2	*cups sour dairy cream*
3/4	*cup sugar*
1/4	*cup all-purpose flour*
1	*teaspoon ground cinnamon*
1/4	*teaspoon ground cloves*
1	*cup raisins*
1/2	*cup pecans, chopped*

Meringue:

3	*egg whites*
1/4	*teaspoon salt*
1/4	*teaspoon cream of tarter*
6	*tablespoons sugar*

Crust:

1. Preheat oven to 450F(230C).

2. In large bowl, mix together flour and salt. Using a pastry blender or 2 knives, cut in shortening until the size of small peas. Sprinkle cold water over mixture, stirring lightly until dough holds together.

3. Shape into a ball, flatten to 1/2-inch thickness. On a lightly floured surface, roll dough into a 9 1/2-inch circle. Press into a 8-inch pie pan. Fold edges and crimp. Prick generously with fork. Bake 10 to 12 minutes. Cool.

(Continued on next page)

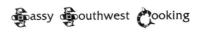

HONDO RAISIN CREAM PIE

(Continued from previous page)

Filling:
1. In top of double boiler, blend egg yolks and sour cream; stir in sugar, flour cinnamon and cloves.

2. Cook over hot water until mixture thickens, stirring occasionally. Stir in raisins and pecans. Cover and cool.

Meringue:
1. Preheat oven to 350F(175C). In a bowl, beat egg whites, salt and cream of tarter until slightly mounding. Gradually beat in sugar. Beat until meringue is stiff and glossy.

Final assembly:
1. Preheat oven to 350F(175C).

2. Turn filling into baked pie shell. Top with meringue, sealing at edge of crust.

3. Bake for 10 to 15 minutes. Cool before serving.

Makes 8-inch pie.

HONEY & SPICE CUPCAKES

Delicious and easy to make, these are a modern
version of an old ranch recipe that was a favorite of
my Uncle Ray.

1/3	*cup butter*
1/2	*cup packed brown sugar*
1	*egg*
3/4	*cup applesauce*
1-1/2	*cups all-purpose flour*
1	*cup rolled oats*
1	*teaspoon ground cinnamon*
1	*teaspoon baking soda*
1	*teaspoon salt*
1/2	*teaspoon ground nutmeg*
1/2	*cup milk*

Honey glaze:

2-1/2	*cups powdered sugar*
2	*tablespoons milk*
1	*teaspoon orange juice*
2	*tablespoons honey*
	coconut

1. Preheat oven to 375F(190C). Grease 12 cup muffin
    tin.

2. In bowl, cream together butter and brown sugar.
    Beat in egg and applesauce.

3. In small bowl, combine flour, oats, cinnamon, soda,
    salt and cinnamon. Blend into creamed mixture
    alternately with milk.

4. Pour batter into prepared cups filling each 3/4 full.
    Bake 20 to 22 minutes. Cool.

5. In small bowl, combine glaze ingredients except
    coconut and beat until smooth. Spread on cupcakes.
    Sprinkle with coconut.

Makes 12 muffins.

*Rolled oats in my recipe refers to old
fashioned oats, not the quick-type.
If you only have the quick-cooking
type they can be substituted.*

LAYERED BANANA & PINEAPPLE TORTILLA

Another example of the versatile tortilla, wafer-like crispness contrasted with two creamy-fruit fillings.

> 5 (8-inch) flour tortillas
> 4 tablespoons butter

Pineapple filling:
> 1 (20-oz.) can crushed pineapple with juice
> 1 tablespoon rum
> 2 egg yolks
> 1 tablespoon cornstarch
> 2 tablespoons sugar
> 1/2 cup roasted almonds, coarsely chopped, blanched

Banana filling:
> 1-1/2 cups whipping cream
> 1 tablespoon rum
> 1/2 cup sugar
> 1/4 cup flour
> 2 whole eggs
> 2 egg yolks
> 2 sliced bananas
> whole strawberries
> whole blanched almonds

1. Preheat oven to 325F(165C). Butter both sides of tortillas. Place on cookie sheets; bake about 20 minutes, until crisp, turning 2 to 3 times. Cool.

Pineapple filling:
2. In a saucepan, combine all ingredients except almonds. Heat slowly to boiling and mixture thickens; continue cooking 3 minutes. Remove and chill. Stir in almonds before using.

Banana filling:
3. In a saucepan bring the cream and rum to a boil. In double boiler, over hot water, beat sugar, flour, eggs and egg yolks, until light. Slowly add cream beating continually until mixture thickens enough to hold its shape. Remove from heat and cover. Chill; add bananas before using.
4. Place a spoonful of banana filling in center of each serving plate; top with a tortilla. Alternate fillings and tortillas, ending with a tortilla on top. Garnish with strawberries and almonds. Serve immediately.

Makes 6 servings.

PECOS VALLEY PUMPKIN PIE

A delicious butterscotch sauce makes this a special treat.

2/3	*cup sugar*
1	*cup cooked pumpkin*
1/4	*teaspoon salt*
1/4	*teaspoon ground ginger*
1/4	*teaspoon ground mace*
1/2	*teaspoon ground cinnamon*
2	*large eggs, beaten slightly*
1	*cup milk*
1	*tablespoon melted butter*

1   *unbaked 8-inch pie crust, (page 150 Hondo Raisin Cream Pie)*

Butterscotch Sauce:

1/2	*cup plus two tablespoons packed brown sugar*
1/3	*cup dark corn syrup*
2	*tablespoons butter*
6	*tablespoons half-and-half*
1	*cup whipped cream*
1/2	*teaspoon vanilla extract*
1/2	*teaspoon rum flavoring*

Filling:

1. Preheat oven to 450F(230C). In large bowl, combine sugar, pumpkin, salt, ginger, mace and cinnamon. Add eggs and mix well. Stir in milk and butter.

2. Pour into unbaked pie crust; bake for 10 to 12 minutes. Reduce heat to 400F(205C); bake for 5 minutes. As crust browns reduce heat to 300F(150C). Bake until knife tip inserted in center comes out clean. Serve with butterscotch sauce.

(Continued on next page)

PECOS VALLEY PUMPKIN PIE

(Continued from preceding page)

Butterscotch Sauce:
1. In saucepan, combine brown sugar, syrup and butter. Bring to a boil, stir constantly until syrup forms a soft ball in cold water. Remove from heat immediately and pour in half & half. Beat thoroughly. Set aside and cool to room temperature.

2. In mixing bowl or copper bowl, whip heavy cream until just stiff. Fold 4 tablespoons of butterscotch sauce into whipped cream; refrigerate remaining sauce, fold in vanilla and rum flavoring. Serve with pie.

PECAN PEACH CAKE

A delicious cake! Roast pecans lend a marvelous flavor. I've always been fond of peaches and this is my all time favorite peach cake.

2	*large peaches, peeled and cut into slices*
3	*tablespoons packed brown sugar*
1	*tablespoon lemon juice*
3	*eggs*
2/3	*cup sugar*
2	*cups pecans, roasted and finely ground*
1/3	*cup all-purpose flour*
1	*teaspoon orange zest*
1/4	*teaspoon salt*
3	*egg whites*
2	*tablespoons unsalted butter, cut into small pieces*
	whipped cream for garnish

1. Preheat over to 350F(175C). Generously butter and lightly flour a 9-1/2-inch springform pan.

2. In a bowl, toss the peaches gently with brown sugar and lemon juice.

3. In another small bowl, beat the eggs and sugar until pale yellow and fluffy. Separately combine pecans, flour, zest and salt. Stir into egg and sugar mixture.

4. Beat egg whites until stiff but not dry, gently fold into batter. Pour into prepared pan.

5. Drain peaches and place in a circle on top of batter; dot with butter.

6. Bake 35 to 40 minutes, or until a wooden pick comes out clean. Cool on rack. Open pan and serve topped with whipped cream.

Makes 8 servings.

RUIDOSO DOWNS PIE

This a New Mexico version of the famous Kentucky Derby Downs pie. A sure way to please your guests before heading to the races.

Crust:
1	*cup all-purpose flour*
1/4	*teaspoon salt*
1/3	*cup shortening*
2 to 3	*tablespoons cold water*

Filling:
1/2	*cup butter*
1	*cup sugar*
1/2	*cup all-purpose flour*
2	*eggs*
1	*teaspoon vanilla extract*
1	*cup semi-sweet chocolate chips*
	whipping cream

Crust:
1. In mixing bowl, mix flour and salt; using a pastry blender or 2 knives, cut in shortening until it resembles a course meal. Add water, mix together. Shape into a ball. Wrap in plastic wrap and refrigerate for at least 20 minutes.

2. Preheat oven to 375F(190C). On a lightly floured surface, roll dough into a 10-inch circle. Pat and fit into a 9-inch pie plate; fold edges and crimp; set aside.

Filling:
3. Beat together remaining ingredients except for whipped cream. Pour into pie crust; bake 30 to 40 minutes. Do not overcook. Cool and serve topped with whipped cream.

8 servings.

RUM APPLE CRISP

Rum and lemon combined with apple create a new flavor sensation.

Topping:

1/2	*cup pecans*
1/3	*cup packed brown sugar*
1/2	*cup all-purpose flour*
1/2	*butter*
1/2	*cup shredded coconut*

Filling:

2	*lbs. cooking apples*
1/2	*cup golden raisins*
1/4	*cup packed brown sugar*
1/4	*cup all-purpose flour*
1/4	*cup rum*
3	*tablespoons lemon juice*
1	*teaspoon grated lemon peel*
	ice cream, whipped cream or sour cream

Crisp Topping:
1. In a food processor or blender, combine nuts and sugar and process well. Add flour and butter; process until well mixed. Stir in coconut; set aside.

Rum Apple Crisp:
1. Preheat oven to 400F(205C). Grease 12 x 9 x 2-inch baking dish.

2. Peel, core and thinly slice apples. In a bowl, toss apples with remaining ingredients except whipped cream. Spoon mixture into prepared baking dish. Cover with crisp topping.

3. Bake 35 to 45 minutes until topping is well browned and bubbling. Serve warm with ice cream, whipped cream or sour cream.

Makes 8 servings.

 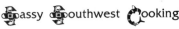

SOPA INDIAN BREAD PUDDING

Here is a very good way to use your stale bread. Like all bread puddings it is very rich and satisfying.

1	*loaf white sandwich bread*
1	*(12-oz.) pkg. American cheese, sliced*
1	*cup pecans, chopped*
1	*(15-oz.) pkg. seedless raisins*
2-1/2	*cups water*
3	*cups packed brown sugar*
1	*tablespoon ground cinnamon*
1/4	*teaspoon ground nutmeg*
1	*tablespoon butter*
	Cream

1. Lightly toast bread and tear in pieces. In a 2-quart baking dish, put a layer of pieces. Place sliced cheese in a layer over bread pieces. Sprinkle pecans and raisins over cheese, fill as full as possible, press down if necessary.

2. Preheat oven to 350F(175C). In a saucepan heat water, brown sugar, cinnamon, nutmeg and butter. Bring to a boil, reduce heat; simmer for 15 minutes. Pour over mixture until all ingredients are soaked and covered. Cover dish with foil; bake for 1 hour. Serve warm or cold, plain or with cream.

Makes 8 servings.

The Spaniards brought a number of items to Native Americans of New Mexico. These include the wheel, metal tools, a written language and gun powder. They changed the Indians diet by introducing fruit trees, wheat, sheep, pigs, horses and many vegetables.

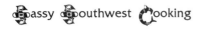

APPENDIX

Southwest Specialty Items
Specialties of New Mexico
1010 South Main
Roswell, NM 88201
505-622-6855
Spices and Gourmet Foods
We Ship Anywhere

Magazine
Chile Pepper Magazine
P.O. Box 4278
Albuquerque, NM 87196
505-266-8322
Published Bi-monthly
6 issues $18.95

Twenty-one Varieties of Beans and One Pea
Gallina Canyon Road
144 Camino Escondido
Santa Fe, NM 87501
Product list available upon request. Send $1.00 and SASE.

Newsletter
The Chile Institute
Box 30003, Dept 3Q
Las Cruces, NM 88003
505-646-5171
Non-profit organization
Devoted to study of Chiles

New Mexico Candies
Senior Murphy, Candymaker
1904 Chamisa Street
P.O.Box 2505
Santa Fe, NM 87504
Candy-Pecans-Pinon Nuts
Price list available upon request.

Fresh/Dry Chiles
Hobson Gardens
3656 E. Hobson Rd.
Roswell, NM 88201
505-622-7289
Red and Green Chiles
Boxing and Shipping Anywhere

Seed Distributors
D.V. Burrell Seed Growers Co.
Rocky Ford Seed House
Box 150
Rocky Ford, CO 81067
719-254-3318
Fax 719-254-3319

Special Thanks To:
La Nell Witt, Ph.D.
Nellie Brito Fields
The Martinez Family
Eve Ware
Edie Hughes

 assy outhwest ooking